Building on Experiences in Adult Development

Betty Menson, *Editor*

NEW DIRECTIONS FOR EXPERIENTIAL LEARNING
Sponsored by the Council for the Advancement of
Experiential Learning (CAEL)

PAMELA J. TATE, *Editor-in-Chief*;
GERARD G. GOLD, *Associate Editor*;
MORRIS T. KEETON, *Consulting Editor*

Number 16, June 1982

Paperback sourcebooks in
The Jossey-Bass Higher Education Series

Jossey-Bass Inc., Publishers
San Francisco • Washington • London

Building on Experiences in Adult Development
Number 16, June 1982
    Betty Menson, *Editor*

New Directions for Experiential Learning Series
Pamela J. Tate, *Editor-in-Chief*
Gerard G. Gold, *Associate Editor*
Morris T. Keeton, *Consulting Editor*

New Directions for Experiential Learning is published quarterly
by Jossey-Bass Inc., Publishers, and is sponsored by the Council
for the Advancement of Experiential Learning (CAEL).

Correspondence:
Subscriptions, single-issue orders, change of address notices,
undelivered copies, and other correspondence should be sent to
New Directions Subscriptions, Jossey-Bass Inc., Publishers,
433 California Street, San Francisco, California 94104.

Editorial correspondence should be sent to the Editor-in-Chief,
Pamela J. Tate or the Consulting Editor, Morris T. Keeton
at the Council for the Advancement of Experiential Learning (CAEL),
Suite 300, Lakefront North, Columbia, Maryland 21044.

Library of Congress Catalogue Card Number LC 81-48569
International Standard Serial Number ISSN 0271-0595
International Standard Book Number ISBN 87589-892-0

Cover art by Willi Baum
Manufactured in the United States of America

Ordering Information

The paperback sourcebooks listed below are published quarterly and can be ordered either by subscription or as single copies.

Subscriptions cost $35.00 per year for institutions, agencies, and libraries. Individuals can subscribe at the special rate of $21.00 per year *if payment is by personal check.* (Note that the full rate of $35.00 applies if payment is by institutional check, even if the subscription is designated for an individual.) Standing orders are accepted.

Single copies are available at $7.95 when payment accompanies order, and *all single-copy orders under $25.00 must include payment.* (California, Washington, D.C., New Jersey, and New York residents please include appropriate sales tax.) For billed orders, cost per copy is $7.95 plus postage and handling. (Prices subject to change without notice.)

To ensure correct and prompt delivery, all orders must give either the *name of an individual* or an *official purchase order number.* Please submit your order as follows:

Subscriptions: specify series and subscription year.
Single Copies: specify sourcebook code and issue number (such as, EL8).

Mail orders for United States and Possessions, Latin America, Canada, Japan, Australia, and New Zealand to:
    Jossey-Bass Inc., Publishers
    433 California Street
    San Francisco, California 94104

Mail orders for all other parts of the world to:
    Jossey-Bass Limited
    28 Banner Street
    London EC1Y 8QE

New Directions for Experiential Learning Series
Pamela J. Tate, *Editor-in-Chief*
Morris T. Keeton, *Consulting Editor*

Contents

Publications Available from CAEL

Assessing Occupational Competences — A CAEL Handbook, Amiel Sharon
College-Sponsored Experiential Learning — A CAEL Handbook, John Duley and Sheila Gordon
College-Sponsored Experiential Learning — A CAEL Student Guide, Hadley and Nesbitt
"Developing and Expanding Cooperative Education," *New Directions for Experiential Learning,* number 2, Pamela J. Tate and Morris T. Keeton, Editors
Efficient Evaluation of Individual Performance in Field Placement, Stephen L. Yelon and John S. Duley
Lifelong Learning: Purposes and Priorities, K. Patricia Cross

Editor's Notes

According to Knefelkamp (1980), "never before in the history of higher education have students and their development been so thoroughly examined." Yet, in spite of this new emphasis on developmental approaches and in spite of the growth of life cycle and adult development theories and research, very few institutions have introduced systems and services for adult learners that reflect what we now know about how adult learners differ from traditional undergraduates.

Thus, this sourcebook has three major purposes: to discuss adult development from a variety of perspectives so as to distinguish the concerns of adult learners from those of traditional students; to help educational practitioners begin to formulate realistic expectations of what educational institutions can and cannot provide for adults; and to present programs and services that reflect an adult development perspective.

Although this sourcebook does include an overview of theories of adult development, it concentrates on practical programming suggestions. This emphasis, in part, is a reflection of my own concerns and experience in the area of adult learning services. Within the last ten years, I have been a returning adult student, a faculty member, and an administrator and coordinator for a consortium of postsecondary institutions exploring assessment of prior learning. In part, however, the emphasis on program strategies is also a response to the needs of practitioners, who tend to have greater experience and interest in applying theory to program development than in refining and elaborating theoretical constructs. In fact, as Cross (1981, p. 153) points out, the current literature on adult development is "faddishly duplicative in some areas (for example, life cycle and needs assessment) and virtually nonexistent in others (for example, the effect of early school experiences on adult attitudes toward learning)."

Although the research is indeed fragmented, one of the most exciting aspects of adult development is that we do not yet have all the answers—that the number of options most adults have about how to live their lives has increased, that in general adults live longer and are more schooled, and that dramatic changes in their lives are possible, even probable. These trends present adult educators with a variety of issues and challenges.

Because of the popularity of books like Sheehy's *Passages* (1976) and Levinson's *Seasons of a Man's Life* (1978), growing familiarity with the theories of Loevinger (1976) and Perry (1970), and the rereading of Erikson (1968) by counselors and educators, many practitioners are con-

1

fused about adult development. Although all theorists seem to be saying that adults change and develop, there are differences that need to be understood if institutional change is to proceed from a clear conceptual framework. In the first chapter, Catherine Marienau and Arthur Chickering explore the central concepts of various schools of adult development theory and discuss the controversies current among them. These authors, who emphasize the need to close the gap between the rhetoric and the reality of our institutional practices, stress that practitioners who advocate institutional change need to understand human development in order to develop effective programs for an increasingly diverse student body.

As most adult educators are aware, the U.S. Census Bureau reports that enrollment of persons over age thirty-five in colleges and universities has increased by 36 percent in the last five years, and half of the people in the twenty-five- to thirty-five-year age group are enrolled in some type of educational program. According to Census Bureau figures, the majority are women enrolled for part-time study. It is important that these women, who make up the greatest proportion of the back-to-school movement, are encouraged to feel more confident, less self-deprecating, more able to cope, less ambivalent. In Chapter Two, Margaret Holt discusses the difficult developmental issues facing re-entry women and the efforts of a voluntary Women's Opportunities Network at the University of Georgia to respond to their special needs and concerns.

While the demand for education today is actually increasing, the demand for traditional education in traditional schools is decreasing rapidly. Professional education for both young and mid-career adults is one of the fastest growing areas of educational demand, and yet, as David Singer points out in Chapter Three, very few professional graduate programs are prepared to respond appropriately to adults. Rarely are adults' prior experiences formally integrated into the process, rarely is affective development consciously fostered, and rarely are professional socialization issues addressed in the curriculum. Although faculties of professional schools sometimes supervise students in internships and practica, they tend to focus on cognitive learning and to neglect the developmental issues that adults are facing as they learn how to be practicing professionals. Singer describes a doctoral program in clinical psychology at Antioch New England that attempts to address adult development and professional socialization issues systematically, and he discusses the implications of this kind of education for the professions.

Although the number of prior learning assessment programs is growing and more credits are being awarded to more adults, the assessment process is still dominated in most institutions by the practical concerns of preparing a portfolio for faculty evaluation and preparing the student to cope with the university. Portfolio development courses are usually the first step in programs that consciously foster personal growth and group support, but many such courses are still oriented toward the mechanics of constructing a portfolio, gathering documentation, and so forth. In Chapter Four, Michael Mark and Betty Menson discuss the impact on adults' cognitive and affective development of introducing David Kolb's experiential learning model and learning style inventory into a portfolio development course at Ohio University. Relying on the reactions of the first hundred adults who took part in the resulting learning style orientation and on the reactions of faculty who evaluated student portfolios, the authors conclude that use of the model and the inventory has had extremely positive effects. The process has increased adults' self-esteem and self-understanding, and higher quality learning outcomes statements are being produced as well.

In the first Bureau of Labor Statistics official bulletin (1977), which analyzed data from the 1970 census, the statement was made that we are fast becoming a nation of career changers. Continuing popularity of Bolles' books (1973, 1978) on career and job change provides further evidence that people in their thirties, forties, and fifties are beginning to be more mobile, to explore a variety of career options, and to realize that they need help with career and education decision making. As colleges and universities have designed programs for adult learners, it is these career changers they have been able to reach most easily—returning women, adults in need of further professional education, people in mid-career transitions. What about the high school dropout who considers enrolling in a GED program, or the blue-collar worker who has been laid off and who needs encouragement to pursue vocational training in a new field? These adults are less often the target of university outreach programs. In Chapter Five, Nina Thomas, Barbara Majnarich, and Dianne Lobes, who have worked successfully with adults in a variety of life circumstances and at every stage of development, describe the counseling strategies developed in their community-based educational brokering center and provide an overview of their center's clients and services.

Chapter Six describes another recent experiment with portfolio development courses at Sinclair Community College in Dayton, Ohio, which has had a large and viable credit for lifelong learning program since 1976. At this institution, the impetus for change was the student attrition rate—almost 50 percent during the first four years of the program's existence. Brenda Krueger attributes the recent sharp drop in student attrition to dramatic changes in the program, which adopted an experiential, holistic, and group process approach to portfolio development. One important step in redesign of the program was to engage faculty and staff in extensive training in the areas of group facilitation skills and holistic education philosophy, which is committed to the development of the total human being—mind, body, spirit, and social responsibility. Krueger highlights the positive changes in faculty who took part in the program, and she describes current plans to integrate holistic education strategies with degree planning.

In Chapter Seven, Pamela Haines and Robert Schwoebel describe a program at Temple University that attempts to foster self-directed learning on the part of service economy workers employed there. The model that these authors present and the issues that they raise about the needs of working adults in today's postindustrial economy are provocative. With changing technology, a reordering of the workplace and our social institutions, and a bewildering array of choices facing adults today, they ask, how can adults be helped to cope with a changing world? What can higher education contribute to adult development in this broader sense? Through the Gateway Seminar, a personalized mentoring system, faculty development workshops, and a variety of noncredit and credit workshops on personal development, career upgrading, and critical thinking skills, the Center for Contemporary Studies at Temple University is trying to address these questions.

In a time of tightening budgets for higher education, it becomes increasingly difficult to introduce services and programs like those described in this sourcebook. The pressure from institutional administrators is often for high enrollment, substantial profit and low attrition in adult learning programs. In such an environment, the fostering of adult development may seem a luxury, not an essential component of programs. But, as all the authors imply, established adult learning programs can be improved at little additional cost. Informal faculty training in adult development, use of volunteer networks, introduction of an inexpensive but effective technique like the Kolb learning style inventory, use of an informal mentoring system—all these techniques can improve adult satisfaction with programs.

If higher education is to compete successfully with other providers of postsecondary education, it must begin to incorporate human development concerns into its planning, its rhetoric, and its services. It is our hope that this sourcebook will supply practitioners with useful, affordable suggestions for improving their programs and give them a better grasp of what an adult development perspective really means in a variety of institutions.

Betty Menson
Editor

References

Bolles, R. *What Color Is Your Parachute?* Berkeley, Calif.: Ten Speed Press, 1973.
Bolles, R. *Three Boxes of Life.* Berkeley, Calif.: Ten Speed Press, 1978.
Bureau of Labor Statistics. *Employment and Earnings.* Washington, D.C.: Bureau of Labor Statistics, 1977.

Chickering, A. W., and Knefelkamp, L. L. *Integrating Adult Development Theory with Higher Education Practice: Current Issues in Higher Education.* Washington, D.C.: American Association for Higher Education, 1980.

Cross, K. P. *Adults as Learners: Increasing Participation and Facilitating Learning.* San Francisco: Jossey-Bass, 1981.

Erikson, E. *Identity: Youth and Crisis.* New York: Norton, 1968.

Levinson, D. J., and others. *The Seasons of a Man's Life.* New York: Knopf, 1978.

Loevinger, J. *Ego Development: Conceptions and Theories.* San Francisco: Jossey-Bass, 1976.

Perry, W. G., Jr. *Forms of Intellectual and Ethical Development in the College Years.* New York: Holt, Rinehart and Winston, 1970.

Sheehy, G. *Passages: Predictable Crises of Adult Life.* New York: Dutton, 1976.

Betty Menson is director of adult learning services at Ohio University. She is CAEL Regional Manager for the Eastern Central Region and a national leader in the development of experiential learning programs. As director of Project Learn for the Central States Region, she is presently coordinating the development of a telecourse on adult life career planning.

Adult development and learning environment
research and theory offer important clues for
closing the gap between rhetoric and reality in
how colleges and universities respond to adult
learners in the 1980s.

Adult Development and Learning

Catherine Marienau
Arthur W. Chickering

Building on the innovative efforts of nontraditional educators during the past two decades, today's adult learning practitioners have available a wealth of experience and resources in tailoring education to the individual, incorporating experiential learning into the curriculum, and delivering teaching and advising at times and places convenient to adults. Despite these efforts, however, relatively few colleges and universities are fully responsive to diverse adult learners, while even in institutions that have attempted to serve adults, "there have been few thoughtful and systematic applications of current theoretical knowledge about adults" (Weathersby and Tarule, 1980, p. 42).

The incongruence between research evidence and practice points out the critical need for creating responsive environments that promote the growth and development of individual adult learners. The time has come to acknowledge and address the role of human development in the academic arena.

The Educative Environment

Let us look more closely at some conceptions, borrowed from Dewey's (1938) "philosophy of educative experience," of an educationally

B. Menson (Ed.). *New Directions for Experiential Learning: Building on
Experiences in Adult Development*, no. 16. San Francisco: Jossey-Bass, June 1982.

and developmentally powerful environment. We rely heavily on Dewey because his thinking about conditions for learning is as germane today as it was some forty years ago. Dewey contends that while "all genuine education comes about through experience," (1938, p. 25) "everything depends on the quality of the experience which is had" (p. 27). According to Dewey, "an experience is always what it is because of a transaction taking place between an individual and what, at the time, constitutes his environment" (1938, p. 43). Working together, continuity, the principle that every experience lives on in further experiences, and interaction, the interplay between objective and subjective conditions, "provide the measure of the educative significance and value of an experience. The immediate and direct concern of an educator is then with the situations in which interaction takes place" (1938, p. 45).

In Dewey's view, it is not specific materials, or methods, or subject matter per se "that is educative or that is conducive to growth" (1938, p. 46). However, failure to adapt these to the needs and capabilities of individuals "may cause an experience to be noneducative quite as much as the failure of the individual to adapt himself to the material" (p. 47). Thus, as Dewey and many adult development theorists tell us, teachers and learners are engaged in a continuous process of reconstructing experience. If that reconstruction process is to be educative, individual learners must be able to interact with their environment in meaningful ways.

Cross (1981) contends that if we are to build truly responsive environments, we need to strengthen our knowledge base and our understanding of the learners themselves. We recall that, on behalf of adult learners, Knowles (1970, 1978), Erikson (1968), Chickering (1976), and Dewey (1938) all stress the role of experience, freedom to make judgments, and responsibility for the consequences of choice and action. Cross encourages us to think further "about the special characteristics of adults and the context in which learning takes place" (1981, p. 234) in her recently developed framework, "Characteristics of Adult Learners (CAL)" (see Figure 1). The learner is described by personal characteristics that represent a continuum of growth along three dimensions: physical, psychological, and sociocultural. Situational characteristics describe the conditions under which learning takes place. Cross emphasizes that "adults are typically part-time learners, and they are usually volunteers" (p. 235).

Each of these personal characteristics continua has a different configuration. Consequently, educators need to think differently about each one. We can think about physiological aging in terms of the three phases of intellectual development described by Schaie and Parr (1981). In this context, the physiological continuum moves from acquisition of skills, to stabilization and integration of skills, to a focus on what is known and instrumental; the trade-off is increased power of intellect for reduced

Figure 1
Characteristics of Adults as Learners (CAL)

Personal Characteristic

···········> Physiological/Aging ···········>
···········> Sociocultural/Life Phases ···········>
···········> Psychological/Developmental Stages ···········>

Situational Characteristics

Part-Time Learning versus Full-Time Learning
Voluntary Learning versus Compulsory Learning

Source: Cross, K. Patricia. *Adults As Learners.* San Francisco: Jossey-Bass, 1981, p. 235.

speed in processing new information. Cross (1981) describes life phases as periods of stability interrupted by transitions. In her view, "one life phase is not higher or better than another, only more appropriate for a given age" (p. 236). The developmental stages continuum also follows a pattern of stability and transition, but in this case the succession of stages is toward greater growth or maturity.

Educational responses to the physiological and sociocultural continua, Cross advises, should be "adaptive and adjustive" (1981, p. 239). Make adjustments for the sensory and physical needs of aging learners and adapt curriculum and learning tasks to capitalize on adults' intelligence. Since transitions can indeed trigger adults' readiness to learn, the educator's response to changing life phases should also be adjustive. As Cross explains, "educators who understand the life phase being left behind and the one to come can design learning experiences to aid in the transition to a new phase of the life cycle" (1981, p. 240).

In the ongoing debate about the hierarchical sequence of adult developmental stages, which will be discussed later in this chapter, an important question emerges for educators: What is the appropriate educational approach to adults vis-à-vis this third developmental stage continuum? Cross is convinced, as are we, that educators should assume a challenger role. "If one accepts a hierarchy of developmental stages, and if one believes that the role of educators is to help each individual develop to the highest possible level, then the role of educators is to challenge the learners to move to increasingly advanced stages of personal development" (Cross, 1981, p. 240).

Effective implementation of the elements from these three personal characteristics continua, Cross suggests, "is not as difficult in practice as it is conceptually" (1981, p. 240). In our work with diverse adult students, most of us tend to respond, at least intuitively, along these lines. Cross encourages us to become more articulate and deliberate in creating environments that are "warm and accepting" on the physiological dimension, "cooperative and adventuresome" on the life phase continuum, and "challenging" on the developmental stage continuum (p. 240). We can be more intentional in building this kind of environment if we incorporate Cross's situational variables (see Figure 1) in our designs. Adult learners should be viewed as part-time learners regardless of their credit load. Very few adults exchange their full-time roles in job and family for that of student. The student role remains secondary, a part-time commitment sandwiched in between other demands. Most adults who continue or resume their formal education do so on the basis of informed thought and choice. In this sense, they participate in education voluntarily, while the attendance of youth is mandatory.

Cross's model, in its early stage of development, incorporates "the major existing theories of adult learning (andragogy and developmental stage and phase theory) into a common framework, and it offers a mechanism for thinking about a growing, developing human being in the context of the special situations common to part-time volunteer learners" (Cross, 1981, p. 243). When we embellish this framework with the details provided by Knowles about learner characteristics and design elements and by Erikson, Chickering, and Dewey about environmental characteristics, we have a powerful guide to facilitate effective learning in an educative environment.

In setting the stage for such an environment for adults, we draw heavily on Knowles' model of "andragogy—the art and science of helping adults [to] learn" (Knowles, 1970, p. 39) and on Erikson's psychosocial model of development (Widick, Parker, and Knefelkamp, 1978).

Andragogy identifies significant characteristics of adult learners and suggests what educators can do to help adults to learn. Against this description, says Cross, "andragogy is probably closer to a theory of teaching than to a theory of learning" (Cross, 1981, p. 227). According to Knowles, "Andragogy is premised on at least four crucial assumptions about the characteristics of adult learners that are different from the assumptions about child learners, on which traditional pedagogy is premised. These assumptions are that, as a person matures, (1) his self-concept moves from one of being a dependent personality toward one of being a self-directing human being, (2) he accumulates a growing reservoir of experience that becomes an increasing resource for learning, (3) his readiness to learn becomes oriented increasingly to the developmental tasks of his social roles, and (4) his time perspective changes from one of postponed application of knowledge to immediacy of application, and accordingly his orientation toward learning shifts from one of subject centeredness to one of problem centeredness" (1970, p. 39). Table 1 summarizes the basic differences between pedagogy and andragogy.

Erikson's elements of an environment that is responsive to adult learners reinforce Knowles's notions about developmental social roles. The climate that Erikson suggests encourages experimentation with varied roles, experience of choice, meaningful achievement, freedom from excessive anxiety, and time for reflection and introspection (Widick, Parker, and Knefelkamp, 1978, p. 14). Chickering integrates major concepts from Knowles and Erikson in his scheme of characteristics of the healthy person and the healthy environment and of the corresponding educational responses (see Table 2).

An overview of research and theory on adult development will help us to construct a solid bridge to practice. The chapter will conclude with a series of questions that can help adult educators to guide their institutions in responding to adult learners.

Table 1. Comparison of Assumptions and
Designs of Pedagogy and Andragogy

	Assumptions			Design Elements	
	Pedagogy	Andragogy		Pedagogy	Andragogy
Self-concept	Dependency	Increasing self-directiveness	Climate	Authority oriented, formal, competitive	Mutuality, respectful, collaborative, informal
Experience	Of little worth	Learners are a rich resource for learning	Planning	By teacher	Mechanism for mutual planning
Readiness	Biological development, social pressure	Developmental tasks of social roles	Diagnosis of needs	By teacher	Mutual self-diagnosis
Time perspective	Postponed application	Immediacy of application	Formulation of objectives	By teacher	Mutual negotiation
Orientation to learning	Subject centered	Problem centered	Design	Logic of the subject matter; content units	Sequenced in terms of readiness; problem units
			Activities	Transmittal techniques	Experiential techniques (inquiry)
			Evaluation	By teacher	Mutual rediagnosis of needs; mutual measurement of program

Source: Knowles, 1978, p. 110.

Table 2. Characteristics of Healthy Person—
Healthy Environment and Educational Responses

Healthy Person	Healthy Environment	Educational Responses
1. Self acceptance; valuing self and others	Recognizes and respects individuals and individual differences	Individualized education; assessment of prior learning
2. Sense of self determination, control, self development	Meaningful achievement regarding personally important purposes	Orientation for goal and value clarification; self assessment; diverse curricular and course alternatives; challenge to think and problem solve
3. Clear and realistic perception of self and environment	Experimentation with varied roles and responsibilities	Varied learning tasks; "extra" curricular activities; sponsored experiential learning
4. Openness to and understanding of and ability to manage emotions	Supportive and energizing human relationships	Whole, teacher-whole students; adult-adult; mentor facilitator, resource; peer relationships, collaborative projects.
5. Capacity to understand, relate to and work with others	Time for assistance with reflection and introspection	One-on-one; support groups; reflective exercises and self evaluation

Source: A.W. Chickering. Handout for the Higher Education for Adult Mental Health Summer Institute, Memphis State University, May 1981.

14

Relationships Between Life Cycle Phases
and Developmental Stages

Some Organizing Themes and Issues. In our view, the purpose of higher education is to help individual learners to understand and direct the changing society in which they live. We believe that higher education should help individuals to satisfy different developmental needs, depending on their place in the life cycle; it should help individuals to manage life transitions and find resources for changing their lives; and it should provide settings to help individuals assemble and change their life structures.

The field of adult development, while relatively new, is growing fast. Multiple schools of thought are emerging, each with its own implications for behaviors and practices in institutions of higher education. Adult development theory is a source of information on what adults "are ready to learn at various times in their lives and how they can be helped to accomplish various developmental tasks" (Cross, 1981, p. 153).

We can begin by establishing working definitions of two basic concepts—*adult* and *adulthood.* Many researchers and practitioners use age as the major identifier of adult status, with ages twenty-two or twenty-five being popular entry points to adulthood. In the context of adult development, we find that age distinction has limited use. It is more fitting to think of adults from a functional point of view (Chickering, 1976). In this sense, an adult is someone who has assumed major responsibilities of adulthood; he or she has gained financial independence from parents or guardians and is operating independently in society. Thus, being an adult is more a function of maturity than of age. Smelser and Erikson (1980) define maturity as the capacity to love and to work. Adulthood, they argue, concerns the processes of adaptation and of change in an individual's life situation over the span of the adult years (p. 6).

Around these definitions revolves a set of complex issues for higher education that are the basis for seven critical questions that Smelser and Erikson raise about the state of adult development theory. These questions stem from the current preoccupation of those in the field with patterns of adaptation and change in adulthood. First, what are the general characteristics of adult transitions? Is there some kind of developmental pattern in adult years? Or are we witness to a parade of life situations that are disjointed and episodic? Second, if there are patterns, how strong are they? Is it possible to identify certain developmental stages that persist despite different life experiences and unique personal histories? Third, is it possible to regard these patterns as a series of distinctive stages? Can they be set apart and bounded? Fourth, if stages of adult development are identified, what are the characteristics and scope of this development?

Fifth, what are the sources of change in adulthood? Are the processes physiological, or is change molded by an individual's changing role relationships throughout the adult years? Is there some kind of psychological process that occurs despite biological and sociocultural constraints? Sixth, can processes of change in adult life be regarded as involving growth, stagnation, deterioration, directionlessness, or perhaps some combination of all these? Seventh, is it possible to evaluate experiences in adulthood? Do we intend to establish levels of experience? Is one kind of adult experience regarded as more creative, fulfilling, or gratifying than another (Smelser and Erikson, 1980, pp. 6-7)?

These issues of individual change and development are at the core both of debate and of agreement in the adult development field. With this in mind, let us examine relationships between two primary aspects of adult development: phases of the life cycle and developmental stages of growth and maturity.

Phases of the Life Cycle. Life cycle theory concerns the "responses people make to age and changing social expectations as they advance through the phases of adulthood" (Cross, 1981, p. 168). Sheehy (1976) popularized the notion that there are predictable turning points in the lives of adults that mark natural passages from one phase to the next. The unfolding of an individual's life cycle over time has been substantiated by research of theorists such as Baltes and Shaie (1973), Gould (1978), Levinson (1978), and Neugarten (1968). Life cycle theorists view adulthood as a time in which change is continuous, interspersed with occasional stable interludes.

Life periods and life structures, central concepts in life cycle theory, have sparked controversy over the use of chronological age as a baseline. A life period is an age-linked period in which certain issues and adaptive tasks are likely to be paramount. Life period supporters (Erikson, 1968; Gould, 1978; Havighurst, 1970) construct charts on phases of the life cycle that assign age boundaries and descriptive labels to each phase. Levinson and his associates (Levinson, 1978; Levinson and others, 1974) have moved away from age-linked periods. Instead, Levinson stresses life structure, "the basic pattern of design of a person's life at a given time" (Weathersby and Tarule, 1980, p. 15). He contends that the place of individuals in the life cycle is influenced most heavily by their social roles in work and intimate relationships. Thus, while both life period and life structure theorists acknowledge common phases in people's lives, life period emphasizes chronological age, and life structure emphasizes external relationships to society.

Theorists and practitioners have found age-linked periods useful in anticipating the "marker events" or transitions that adults can encounter at certain points in their lives: leaving home around age twenty, reexamining commitments around age thirty, becoming one's own person around age forty, redirecting life goals around age fifty, restabilizing one's life around age sixty, and reviewing life around age seventy (Chickering and Havighurst, 1981; Weathersby and Tarule, 1980). However, practitioners' experiences with life cycle theory in designing programs for adult learners suggest that chronological age is a weak indicator of what adults want and need from their educational experiences. Rather, these educators advise that programs be designed around specific tasks embedded in social roles (Lindquist and Marienau, 1981; Marienau, forthcoming). While we need not totally abandon age-linked periods, we should recognize that age linkings are not prescriptive. Cross (1981) is helpful on this matter with her descriptions of life cycle phases (see Table 3).

The concept of marker events or transitions forms a useful bridge to life structure and developmental tasks. Levinson (1978) emphasizes the evolving nature of adulthood, in which the individual life structure creates a space to examine personality, career, socialization, and marker events. The life structure, then, consists of a series of alternating periods of stability and transition. The stable period, which seems to last six or seven years, is a time of structure building (Weathersby and Tarule, 1980). The transition period, which can last four to five years, is a time of structure changing, for this period terminates the existing life structure and creates the possibility for a new one, which is then built around marker events and crucial choices. These choices can involve developmental tasks in the process of adaptation, transition, and growth, a new way of making sense of the world.

Adaptation marks the individual's ability to cope with events created by one's personality or by external forces. Transitions involve the process of coping, either by changing roles or by reconstructing personal philosophies. Timing is a critical prompter of transitions. When transitional events are "on time," Neugarten points out (1968), they are usually anticipated and less likely to be experienced as crises. "'On time' relates to that clock within us and a sense of 'proper' age for events to occur" (Weathersby and Tarule, 1980, p. 10). But, work and child-rearing patterns are changing, "creating a much wider variation in timetables and thus a need to recognize new age norms" (p. 10). Whether transitional events are "on time" or not, Erikson (1968) suggests that developmental crisis can be a constructive turning point. This striving to maintain an equilibrium or "goodness of fit" (Levinson, 1978; Levinson and others, 1974) between the life structure and one's inner sense of experience characterizes life's transitions.

With the process of coping with transitions comes the potential for growth. Gould (1978) emphasizes that growth involves inner changes in consciousness. These changes result from attempts to dissolve illusions from childhood that are ill-fated in the adult world. Like transition, the act of "transformation" "involves a thoughtful confrontation with the reality of one's own choices and experiences" (Weathersby and Tarule, 1980, p. 18).

Thus, the concepts of life structure and developmental tasks link theories of the life cycle and developmental stages. Life cycle periods involve the processes of adaptation, transition, and growth; developmental stages involve the "successive transformations in adults' more inward ways of constructing experience" (Weathersby and Tarule, 1980, p. 22).

Developmental Stages of Growth and Maturity. Developmental stages describe the frame of reference that individuals have for creating and maintaining meaning in their lives. Erikson (1968) and Gould (1978) make certain assumptions about an orderliness of social involvements in work and intimate relationships that parallel the phases of adult development.

Erikson's eight psychosocial tasks deal with the orderly resolution of conflicts (Widick, Parker, and Knefelkamp, 1978). In the evolution of adulthood, these conflicts oppose intimacy to isolation in young adulthood, generativity to stagnation in middle adult years, and integrity to despair in the later years. An attitude of wholeness results from resolution of these related concerns. Gould's (1978) conception of life transformation also connotes progression. He emphasizes the individual's movement from childhood dependency to a state of liberation gained by challenging assumptions and myths throughout life.

The hierarchy implied in these approaches and in the approaches of others (Kohlberg, 1973; Loevinger, 1976; Perry, 1970, 1981) suggests that it is better to be at a higher level or position of ego, moral, or intellectual development than at a lower level. However, both Loevinger (1976) and Weathersby (1981) express reservations about the validity of the hierarchy concept, pointing out that higher stages do not necessarily bring about happiness or better adjustment to society (Cross, 1981). The debate centers on whether stages are hierarchical movements characterized by developmental stages that bring more satisfaction or constant successions with their own developmental tasks. Whichever position one adopts, there is general agreement that development is identifiable as a series of stable periods linked by transitions and that it involves a life structure that has ego, moral, and cognitive dimensions.

These dimensions are a composite of individual development, which involves constructing and searching for the deeper meaning of experiences (ego development); reflecting, examining, and making judgments about moral questions (moral development), and developing and strengthening intellectual competence (intellectual development). Loevinger (1976), the leading theorist in ego development, considers this domain "to be not just a personality trait, but a master trait second only to intelligence in determining an individual's pattern of response to situations" (Weathersby and Tarule, 1980, p. 26).

Table 3. Descriptions of Life-Cycle Phases

Phase and Age	Marker Events	Psychic Tests	Characteristic Stance
Leaving Home 18-22	Leave home Establish new living arrangements Enter college Start first full-time job Select mate	Establish autonomy and independence from family Define identity Define sex role Establish new peer alliances	A balance between "being in" and "moving out" of the family
Moving into Adult World 23-28	Marry Establish home Become parent Get hired/fired/quit job Enter into community activities	Regard self as adult Develop capacity for intimacy Fashion initial life structure Build the dream Find a mentor	"Doing what one should" Living and building for the future Launched as an adult
Search for Stability 29-34	Establish children in school Progress in career or consider change Possible separation, divorce, remarriage Possible return to school	Reappraise relationships Reexamine life structure and present commitments Strive for success Search for stability, security, control Search for personal values Set long-range goals Accept growing children	"What is this life all about now that I am doing what I am supposed to?" Concern for order and stability and with "making it" Desire to set long-range goals and meet them

Stage / Age			
Becoming One's Own Person 37-42	Crucial promotion Break with mentor Responsibility for three-generation family; i.e., growing children and aging parents For women: empty nest; enter career and education	Face reality Confront mortality; sense of aging Prune dependent ties to boss, spouse, mentor Reassess marriage Reassess personal priorities and values	Suspended animation More nurturing stance for men; more assertive stance for women "Have I done the right thing? Is there time to change?"
Settling Down 45-55	Cap career Become mentor Launch children; become grandparents New interests and hobbies Physical limitations; menopause Active participation in community events	Increase feelings of self-awareness and competence Reestablish family relationships Enjoy one's choices and life style Reexamine the fit between life structure and self	"It is perhaps late, but there are things I would like to do in the last half of my life" Best time of life
The Mellowing 57-64	Possible loss of mate Health problems Preparation for retirement	Accomplish goals in the time left to live Accept and adjust to aging process	Mellowing of feelings and relationships Spouse increasingly important Greater comfort with self
Life Review 65 +	Retirement Physical decline Change in finances New living arrangements death of friends/spouse Major shift in daily routine	Search for integrity versus despair Acceptance of self Disengagement Rehearsal for death of spouse	Review of accomplishments Eagerness to share everyday human joys and sorrows Family is important Death is a new presence

Sources: From, Cross, 1981, pp. 174-175.

Ego Development. Each stage of ego development constitutes qualitatively different ways of responding to life experience (Weathersby, 1981). Two concepts associated with life cycle periods—turning points and marker events or highlights—also are related to personality development. Loevinger's (1976) scheme of ego development entails a sequence of turning points that she calls "milestone sequences." These milestone sequences "represent broad patterns of change involving many aspects of personality" (Weathersby and Tarule, 1980, p. 26). Marker events—crises that cause anxiety and give rise to the ego's major task, establishing coherent meaning in experience (Erikson, 1968)—are a major impetus for change. Changes in developmental stages require some change in related areas, as depicted in Table 4. The distinctions highlighted in Table 4 illustrate that particular traits can be more or less pronounced, depending on where individuals are in their stage of development.

Four points need to be stressed in these conceptions of ego development, including moral and intellectual development. First, the dynamics involved in transition from one stage to the next are more representative of an individual's development than is the individual's place in any one of the hierarchical stages. Loevinger (1976) views ego development on a continuum, stressing the process rather than the state of development. Perry (1981), too, notes that, with regard to moral and intellectual development, the drama is in the transition. Second, stages are additive. As individuals move from one stage to the next, they bring with them the insight acquired in prior stages. Third, achievement is interpreted as the ability to cope with increasingly complex problems, not as success in problem resolution. The "Is higher better?" issue resurfaces. Loevinger (1976) urges us to recognize that emotional independence is an issue at all stages and that it is possible for people to be well adjusted at all but perhaps the lowest levels. Fourth, age and stage are not highly correlated. Age is a chronological marker for periods in the individual's life cycle; stage of development indicates the level at which individuals construct meaning out of life experiences.

Moral Development. In his early research, Kohlberg (1969) "constructed moral dilemmas that placed socially accepted values in conflict . . . and set out to determine how these conflicts would be understood and resolved" (Gilligan, 1981, p. 142). On the basis of findings from this and later investigations, Kohlberg described six stages of moral development, which centered on "the concept of conventional morality" (Gilligan, 1981, p. 142). Kohlberg and other theorists have grappled with how and to what extent moral judgment is transformed by adult experience. As a result, the conceptualization of moral development has shifted "from moral ideology to ethical responsibility . . . accompanied by a change in concern from issues of identity to those of intimacy" (Gilligan, 1981, p. 155). Moral development thus involves the broader domain of interpersonal competence and concerns individuals' capacity to work and to love throughout their treatments of personal and ethical issues (Smelser and Erikson, 1980; Torbert, 1981).

For adults, issues of moral development center on the quality of human interaction and the interdependence of the self and others. The problem of moral judgment is confronted when individuals turn their reflective thought inward to examine their own constructions and their responses to experience. Torbert (1981) suggests that learning from experience follows an "inquiring strategy." The capacity to discern the moral problem (reflective thought) and the capacity to remain responsive to the reality of experience link the separate strains of intellectual and moral development (Gilligan, 1981; Perry, 1981).

Intellectual Development. Some theorists (Baltes and Schaie, 1973; Perry, 1970) have looked at intellectual development as separate from ego and moral development. Intellectual development is not to be confused with intelligence. Rather it concerns intellectual competence—the active use of intellect in specific situations.

Schaie and Parr (1981) describe three distinct phases of intellectual development. Phase one emphasizes the attainment of intellectual skills and their application to personal and societal goals. This phase occurs during the late teens and early twenties, during which time skill development takes place in the many aspects of problem finding, problem solving, and evaluation. Phase two involves stabilization and integration of these skills. This second phase, which lasts from middle age to early old age, involves some trade-off between well-developed thought processes and reduced response speed and perceptual processes. In phase three, interests narrow, and attention is focused on what is familiar and meaningful to the individual's life structure. This phase, which occurs in old age, involves a shift in concern from what the individual should know to why he or she should know it.

Two points about intellectual development are worth emphasizing here. Individual variability in almost every type of intellectual capacity increases across the life span. Consequently, we see a greater range of differences in adulthood (Baltes and Schaie, 1973; Cross, 1976, 1979, 1981; Messick and Associates, 1976). Appropriate challenges under adequate conditions can stimulate intellectual growth in the adult years (Perry, 1981). Thus, the challenges and the conditions should be construed to accommodate the learning styles, orientations, and needs of individual adult learners (Cross, 1981).

Development in Adulthood and Implications for Higher Education

We can now better understand that significant development in adulthood is possible, but it is not easy. In Piaget's terms, there is poten-

Table 4. Some Milestones of Ego Development

Stage	Impulse Control, Character Development	Interpersonal Style	Conscious Preoccupation	Cognitive Style
Impulsive	Impulsive, fear of retaliation	Receiving, dependent, expoitative	Bodily feelings, especially sexual and aggressive	Sterotyping, conceptual confusion
Self-Protective	Fear of being caught, externalizing blame, opportunistic	Wary, manipulative, exploitative	Self-protection, trouble, wishes, things, advantage control	
Conformist	Conformity to external rules, shame, guilt for breaking rules	Belonging, superficial niceness	Appearance, social acceptability, banal feelings, behavior	Conceptual simplicity, stereotypes, cliches
Conscientious-Conformist (Self-Aware)	Differentiation of norms, goals	Aware of self in relation to group, helping	Adjustment, problems, reasons, opportunities (vague)	Multiplicity
Conscientious	Self-evaluated standards, self-criticism, guilt for consequences, long-term goals and ideals	Intensive, responsible, mutual, concern for communication	Differentiated feelings, motives for behavior, self-respect, achievements, traits, expression	Conceptual complexity, ideals of patterning

		Add: Distinction of process and outcome	Increased conceptual complexity, complex patterns, toleration for ambiguity, broad scope, objectivity
		Add: Development, social problems, differentiation of inner life from outer	Vividly conveyed feelings, integration of physiological and psychological, psychological causation of behavior, role conception, self-fulfillment, self in social context
			Add: Identity
			Add: Identity
Individualistic	*Add:* Respect for individuality	*Add:* Dependence as an emotional problem	*Add:* Respect for autonomy, interdependence
Autonomous	*Add:* Coping with conflicting inner needs, toleration	*Add:* Respect for autonomy, interdependence	*Add:* Cherishing individual
Integrated	*Add:* Reconciling inner conflicts, reunciation of unattainable	*Add:* Reconciling inner conflicts, reunciation of unattainable	*Add:* Cherishing individual

Note: "*Add*" means in addition to the description applying to the previous level.

Source: Adapted from *Ego Development: Conceptions and Theories*, by Jane Loevinger (San Francisco: Jossey-Bass, 1976) pp. 24-25. Reprinted by permission of Jossey-Bass.

tial for adults to reach a "fifth cognitive stage" that involves problem-creating; many adults, however, do not fully achieve the previous stage's problem-solving ability (Weathersby and Tarule, 1980, p. 37). Kohlberg (1973) asserts that, in his scheme of moral development, the average adult has a Stage Four orientation to authority and maintaining social order. According to Loevinger (1976), the average American adult is a conscientious conformist—in transition between Stage Three and Stage Four.

Two themes recur in these concepts of development in adulthood—transitions and marker events. Transition is indeed the drama of developmental change. It takes will and courage (Perry, 1981) to leave the familiar and comfortable to accept challenge and risk. Transitions can be constructive experiences if we have the will to create or accept marker events that produce just enough disequilibrium to ease the way. However, certain marker events, such as unanticipated death, divorce, and failure to make the grade in job or school, can challenge our equilibrium so deeply that we become paralyzed. In some instances, recognizing the need to move ahead and to change can even enhance the trauma. Individuals look for balance between stability and transition, between what is known and what is sought. They seek some type of blueprint that will help them to make meaning out of life experiences.

Formal education, whether consciously or not, "is a developmental intervention in adults' lives, an activity that is by its very nature linked to processes of growth, development, change, and transformation" (Weathersby and Tarule, 1980, p. 43). And, we do now have significant clues to the differences among adult students. Table 5 shows a progression of individuals' views on knowledge—what it is, its uses, and its sources—and the relation to motives for education. It also illustrates corresponding institutional functions, learning processes, and roles of teachers and learners.

The progression depicted in Table 5 is one of movement toward self-directedness and self-evaluation as individuals assume increasing responsibility for creating significant meaning out of their educational and life experiences. We see, then, some general implications for ways in which higher education institutions could accommodate adults' learning needs and interests. We begin to have a general framework for identifying conditions that are conducive to individuals' growth and development.

What, then, do we do as teachers and administrators to move from rhetoric to reality? We resist drawing up a list of general recommendations, because we find an abundance of them in the literature and a void of research in the field. Instead, we pose the following questions, which have emerged from the concepts and principles that we have sketched in this chapter and from the contributions of practitioners, including Clark (1981), Greenberg (1980), Lehmann and Lester (1978), Lindquist and

Marienau (1981), Marienau (forthcoming), and Weathersby and Tarule (1980). We anticipate that some of these questions could become the basis of criteria that institutions would adapt to their own situations and translate into appropriate actions.

To what extent and in what ways does your institution

Developmental Goals

- Articulate human development as a legitimate outcome of higher education?
- Accommodate a wide variety of learner motivations, life transitions, and developmental stages?

Learning

- Recognize adults' prior experiences as a rich resource for new learning?
- Recognize the diversity of learning styles among adults?
- Provide enabling and flexible arrangements that maximize individualized learning?

Curriculum

- Support field experiences, internships, and so forth as a significant complement to conventional subject matter?
- Define teaching as a facilitating-mentoring function?
- Engage learners in the formulation and clarification of educational and career-life goals?
- Incorporate academic advisors as members of the instructional team?
- Provide a range of access options through flexible approaches to how, when, where, and with whom learning take place?
- Offer programs in convenient locations and under appropriate physical conditions?
- Offer various learning packages through different technologies, such as print, video and television, computer?
- Provide counseling and advising by persons knowledgeable about adults' needs and interests
- Make the individual learner feel cared for and valued as a human and as a consumer?

Faculty and Staff

- Encourage faculty and staff to be informed about adult development and learning?
- Reward faculty for good teaching of adults?

These criteria, while not exhaustive, represent the kinds of considerations that we need to make in creating educational environments that result in meaningful learning.

Table 5. Implications of Ego Stage for Adult Education

Ego Development	What is knowledge?	What use is knowledge?	Where does knowledge come from?	Motive for education
Self-Protective	A possession which helps one to get desired ends; ritualistic actions which yield solutions	Means to concrete ends; used to obtain instrumental effects in world; education to *get X*	From external authority; from asking how to get things	Instrumental; to satisfy immediate needs
Conformist	General information required for social roles; objective truth, revealed by Authority	Social approval, appearance, status used to meet expectations and standards of significant others; education to *be X*	From external authority; from asking how things work	To impress significant others; to gain social acceptance and entry into social roles
Conscientious	Know-how; Personal skills in problem solving; divergent views resolved by rational processes	Competence in work and social rules; used to achieve internalized standards of excellence and to act on or change world; education to *do x*	Personal integration of information based on rational inquiry; from setting goals, exploring causal relationships and asking why things work	To achieve competence relative to standards of excellence
Autonomous	Personally generated insight about self and nature of life; subjective and dialectical; contradiction and paradox as central	Self-knowledge; self development; used to transform self and the world; education to *become x*	Personal experience and reflection; personally generated paradigms, insights, judgments; from asking if things are as they appear	To deepen understanding of self, world, and life cycle; develop increasing capacity to manage own destiny

	Institutional Function	Learning Process	Teacher Role	Student Role
Self-protective	To enforce learning by providing examples, showing how things should be done	*Demonstration:* showing how to	*Enforcer:* Teacher as agent who focuses attention and shows how; focus: showing	Student acts as imitator of activity
Conformist	Provide pre-packaged general experience or basic information; to certify level of information internalization	*Revelation:* of truth by expert authority; if conflict between ideas is perceived, one element is incorrect	*Instructor:* Teacher as presenter of information (often in impersonal group mode, e.g. lecture); focus: verbal presentation	Student as subordinate in frequently impersonal relation with teacher, student internalizes and parrots information
Conscientious	To provide structured programs which offer concrete skills and information, opportunities for rational analysis, and practice, which can be evaluated and certified	*Discovery* of correct answer through scientific method and logical analysis; multiple views acknowledged but congruence and simplicity sought	*Role Model and Evaluator:* Teacher models skills, poses questions, outlines forms of discourse, evaluates analytic abilities and skill competencies; focus: apprenticeship, internship	Student as subordinate in substantial personal interaction with teacher; student analyzes and critiques information, practices competence
Autonomous	To provide new experiences, to ask key questions; to pose key dilemmas; to foster personal experience and personally generated insight; to highlight significant discontinuities and paradoxes	*Emerging levels of insight:* learning entails reorganizing past insight into new personally generated paradigms through new experiences. Learning follows dialectical process in which contradiction and multiplicity of views itself is of interest	*Facilitator:* Teacher sets up experience and reflective observation by students, is a resource for planning and evaluation; focus: facilitating	Student defines purposes in collegial relationship with teacher as equal participant; emphasis is on personal experience, creating own interpretations and meanings, transforming meanings

Source: Harry M. Lasker and Cynthia DeWindt, "Implications of Ego Stage for Adult Development" (Cambridge, Mass.: Harvard Graduate—School of Education, 1976). (Mimeographed.)

28

Conclusion

We now raise two final issues. One issue concerns the need for approaching structural and procedural changes in as organized and integrated a manner as possible within programs or throughout institutions. While improvements often must be tackled in small pieces, "we cannot be satisfied with a few new approaches or altered practices. Tantalizing options for learning may be available in a few areas, while major restrictions persist in others. In too many cases, then, we have managed only to bring students a bit further along in the system before they encounter severe blocks to achieving their full potential" (Lindquist and Marienau, 1981, p. 107).

The second issue concerns the overall aim of the learning society to develop "lifelong learners who possess the basic skills for learning plus the motivation to pursue a variety of learning interests throughout their lives" (Cross, 1981, p. 249). If we want to go beyond helping students to "develop the taste for good learning" (p. 250), we need to provide proper occasions and tools that enable them to advance in intellectual and ethical problem solving. In our efforts to build educative environments, we can move from rhetoric into practice and have powerful makings of a learning society.

References

Baltes, P., and Schaie, K. W. (Eds.). *Life Span Developmental Psychology: Personality and Socialization.* New York: Academic Press, 1973.
Chickering, A. W. "Development as a Major Outcome." In M. T. Keeton and Associates, *Experiential Learning: Rationale, Characteristics, and Assessment.* San Francisco: Jossey-Bass, 1976.
Chickering, A. W. "Characteristics of a Healthy Person—Healthy Environment and Educational Responses." Unpublished presentation to the Higher Education for Adult Mental Health Summer Institute, Memphis State University, May 1981.
Chickering, A. W., and Havighurst, R. J. "The Life Cycle." In A. W. Chickering and Associates, *The Modern American College: Responding to the New Realities of Diverse Students and a Changing Society.* San Francisco: Jossey-Bass, 1981.
Clark, T. "Individualized Education." In A. W. Chickering and Associates, *The Modern American College: Responding to the New Realities of Diverse Students and a Changing Society.* San Francisco: Jossey-Bass, 1981.
Cross, K. P. *Accent on Learning: Improving Instruction and Reshaping the Curriculum.* San Francisco: Jossey-Bass, 1976.
Cross, K. P. "Adult Learners: Characteristics, Needs and Interests." In R. E. Peterson and Associates, *Lifelong Learning in America: An Overview of Current Practices, Available Resources, and Future Prospects.* San Francisco: Jossey-Bass, 1979.
Cross, K. P. *Adults as Learners: Increasing Participation and Facilitating Learning.* San Francisco: Jossey-Bass, 1981.

Dewey, J. *Experience and Education.* New York: Collier Books, 1938.

Erikson, E. *Identity: Youth and Crisis.* New York: Norton, 1968.

Gilligan, C. "Moral Development." In A. W. Chickering and Associates, *The Modern American College: Responding to the New Realities of Diverse Students and a Changing Society.* San Francisco: Jossey-Bass, 1981.

Gould, R. L. *Transformations: Growth and Change in Adult Life.* New York: Simon & Schuster, 1978.

Greenberg, E. "Designing Programs for Learners of All Ages." In E. Greenberg, K. O' Donnell, and W. Bergquist (Eds), *New Directions for Higher Education: Educating Learners of All Ages,* no. 29. San Francisco: Jossey-Bass, 1980.

Havighurst, R. "Changing Status and Roles During the Adult Life Cycle: Significance for Adult Education." In H. W. Burns (Ed.), *Sociological Backgrounds of Adult Education.* New York: Center for the Study of Liberal Education for Adults, Syracuse University, 1970.

Knowles, M. *The Modern Practice of Adult Education: Andragogy Versus Pedagogy.* New York: Association Press, 1970.

Knowles, M. *The Adult Learner: A Neglected Species.* (2nd ed.) Houston: Gulf, 1978.

Kohlberg, L. "Stage and Sequence: The Cognitive-Developmental Approach to Socialization." In D. A. Goslin (Ed.), *Handbook of Socialization Theory and Research.* Chicago: Rand McNally, 1969.

Kohlberg, L. "Continuities in Childhood and Adult Moral Development Revisited." In P. B. Baltes and L. R. Goulet (Eds.), *Life Span Developmental Psychology: Research and Theory.* New York: Academic Press, 1973.

Lehmann, T., and Lester, V. "Adult Learning in the Context of Adult Development: Life Cycle Research and Empire State College Students." Working paper, Empire State College research series, Empire State College, 1978.

Levinson, D. J., and others. *The Seasons of a Man's Life.* New York: Knopf, 1978.

Levinson, D. J., Darrow, C., Klein, E. B., Levinson, M., and McKee, B. "The Psychological Development of Men in Early Adulthood and the Mid-Life Transition." In D. F. Ricks, A. Thomas, and M. Roof (Eds.), *Life History Research in Psychopathology.* Minneapolis: University of Minnesota Press, 1974.

Lindquist, J., and Marienau, C. *Turning Colleges Toward Adults: Bridging Theory and Practice and Adult Development and Planned Changes—Case Study in Higher Education.* Memphis, Tenn.: Institute for Academic Improvement, Center for the Study of Higher Education, Memphis State University, 1981.

Loevinger, J. *Ego Development: Conceptions and Theories.* San Francisco: Jossey-Bass, 1976.

Marienau, C. "Relationships Between Theory and Practice in Adult Development and Planned Change: Case Studies in Higher Education." Unpublished doctoral dissertation, University of Minnesota, forthcoming.

Messick, S., and Associates. *Individuality in Learning: Implications of Cognitive Styles and Creativity for Human Development.* San Francisco: Jossey-Bass, 1976.

Neugarten, B. L. "Adult Personality: Toward a Psychology of the Life Cycle." In B. L. Neugarten (Ed.), *Middle Age and Aging.* Chicago: University of Chicago Press, 1968.

Perry, W. G., Jr. *Forms of Intellectual and Ethical Development in the College Years.* New York: Holt, Rinehart and Winston, 1970.

Perry, W. G., Jr. "Cognitive and Ethical Growth: The Making of Meaning." In A. W. Chickering and Associates, *The Modern American College: Responding* to the New Realities of Diverse Students and a Changing Society. San Francisco, Jossey-Bass, 1981.

Schaie, K. W., and Parr, J. "Intelligence." In A. W. Chickering and Associates, The Modern American College: Responding to the New Realities of Diverse Students and a Changing Society. San Francisco, Jossey-Bass, 1981.

Sheehy, G. Passages: Predictable Crises of Adult Life. New York: Dutton, 1976.

Smelser, N., and Erikson, E. (Eds.). Themes of Work and Love in Adulthood. Cambridge, Mass.: Harvard University Press, 1980.

Torbert, W. R. "Interpersonal Competence." In A. W. Chickering and Associates, The Modern American College: Responding to the New Realities of Diverse Students and a Changing Society. San Francisco, Jossey-Bass, 1981.

Weathersby, R. "Ego Development." In A. W. Chickering and Associates, The Modern American College: Responding to the New Realities of Diverse Students and a Changing Society. San Francisco, Jossey-Bass, 1981.

Weathersby, R. R., and Tarule, J. M. Adult Development: Implications for Higher Education. AAHE-ERIC/Higher Education Research Report, No. 4. Washington, D.C.: American Association for Higher Education, 1980 (ED 191 382).

Widick, C., Parker, C., and Knefelkamp, L. "Erik Erikson and Psychosocial Development." In L. Knefelkamp, C. Widick, and C. Parker (Eds.), New Directions for Student Services: Applying New Developmental Findings, No. 4. San Francisco: Jossey-Bass, 1978.

Catherine Marienau is director of the University Without Walls program at the University of Minnesota. She received a Bush Leadership Fellows award and served as professional-in-residence at the Center for the Study of Higher Education at Memphis State University (1980–81). She is coauthor of two monographs, Turning Colleges Toward Adults and Adult Baccalaureate Programs.

Arthur W. Chickering is Distinguished Professor of Higher Education and director of the Center for the Study of Higher Education at Memphis State University. He is author of Experience and Learning (Change Magazine Press) and editor of The Modern American College: Responding to the New Realities of Diverse Students and a Changing Society (Jossey-Bass, 1981). A member of the original steering committee for the Council for the Advancement of Experiential Learning (CAEL), he is now chairman of the board.

If higher education is to attract and serve returning women, services and programs need to be re-evaluated by administrators, faculty, and student services staffs. One successful program is the Women's Opportunities Network at the University of Georgia.

Designing Programs for Returning Women Students

Margaret Holt

As Margolis (1974, p. 34) notes, "until 1972, the Bureau of the Census didn't count those over thirty-four attending college." Today, the registrars of most higher education institutions in the United States are keenly aware that there are many students over thirty and that the majority of these students are women. It is now common to find on many campuses an official or unofficial group of people specifically interested in assisting mid-life women with their adjustment to student life.

Each time that a group of people comes together in an academic setting to discuss or prepare a program for women beyond age thirty, its members struggle to find a suitable làbel for this clientele. Consensus never comes in this title search. *Re-entry* reminds some of returning astronauts, *nontraditional* evokes images of former homemakers in go-go boots and adda beads, and *older-than-average* smacks of discovering your mother working at McDonalds. Furthermore, if the number of so-called nontraditional students continues to increase at its present rate, it soon will be reasonable to argue that the younger students are the nontraditional ones.

Higher education administrators, faculty, and student service staff preparing their institution to manage the arrival of older women on campus should ask three questions: First, are these individuals so unlike

B. Menson (Ed.). *New Directions for Experiential Learning: Building on Experiences in Adult Development*, no. 16. San Francisco: Jossey-Bass, June 1982.

younger students that costly and time-consuming planning and implementation of new or redesigned programs and services is warranted? Second, if they are, what new programs and services can be developed? Third, what new programs and services are proving beneficial in helping older women students to pursue education?

Physical, Social, and Psychological Characteristics of Mid-Life Women

Life cycle research, which is frequently based on a small sample of men, mostly clinical and descriptive in nature (Cytrynbaum and others, 1980), and very rarely longitudinal, has just begun to identify some of the changes that people undergo as they pass through the adult life span. Although theorists acknowledge that there are differences between men and women, researchers have paid little attention to age and gender. Physical differences are most immediately relevant to those who work in physical education and health services; they involve such issues as maternal health care, menopause, nutrition, fitness, weight control, stress, fatigue, and depression. It is much more likely that younger women students will seek birth control information and assistance than their older counterparts and that older women will express concerns about menopause that are unimportant to the younger women.

Gutmann, Grunes, and Griffin (1980) have investigated gender reversal and cite cross-cultural support for their finding that women normally adopt a more masculine stance as they age. These authors find some evidence in their work in psychiatry that older women who attempt to resist their own emerging assertiveness and masculine qualities sometimes experience depression, guilt, and low self-esteem. Renewed desires to resume a study program can be one result of this shift from relatively passive to relatively active behavior for some mid-life women.

Many adult women exhibit the importance that their return to higher education holds for them in rather pronounced ways. They are frequently described as "excessively serious" students, sometimes "overly driven to high achievement." Sometimes, their drive is greatly admired by their teachers; sometimes, their intensity is criticized or even ridiculed. They often view a return to school as the last chance for personal and professional recognition. Unlike their younger counterparts, it is likely that they will have a specific job or career in mind. It goes almost without saying that their grade point averages are generally high. Certain returning women students with very high expectations express bitterness when they discover that the higher education program that they have entered does not meet the high academic standards that they expected to see observed there (Margolis, 1974). Less serious, younger students are sometimes annoyed by the competition and experiences that these older women bring to the classroom. Unlike younger students, who are dating and fraternizing over weekends, many older women students can be found in the libraries or at home, anxiously reading everything listed in their bibliographies. Academic advisors and counselors find it a challenge to help some returning women students to relax when they initiate their studies. Most returning women students do discover that they can manage the assignments and pass the tests, yet their self-expectations remain rigorous. The thought of failure continues to prevail long after the first-quarter term papers and reports have been evaluated and the excellence of their performance has been recognized.

It is important to understand the motivations for the return to school. Motivations vary from one individual to another, and despite the hypothesis that many adults are returning because of a mid-life crisis of sorts, it is more accurate to describe most of the returning as a mid-life transition. Certainly, many divorced and widowed women have resumed a degree program as a direct result of their changed marital status. Others believe that educational credentials will be necessary for the type of employment that they must have to help their families meet the ever-inflating costs in today's economy. Some women purposely delay their return to school until certain marker events occur—for example, all children are in school, or their last living parent dies. The death of significant others, incidentally, is reported to be one of the central triggers for many mid-life transitions (Cytrynbaum and others, 1980).

The importance of such life events for adults was recently addressed by Aslanian and Brickell (1980). They surveyed 2,000 adults twenty-five years of age and older to gather information about the circumstances that motivate adult learning. Their findings indicate that much adult learning is stimulated by major life transitions, such as moving to a new location or getting married. A sensitive, adaptable, and innovative adult educator can use the significance of these individual life changes in a variety of ways to enhance the learning activities of those in transition.

Other social and psychological factors that influence re-entry for women are the departure of children from the home (the so-called empty-nest period) and a deep concern for the maintenance of attractiveness and youthfulness. It needs to be emphasized, however, that living with adolescent and older children at mid-life has been found to be stress-producing for many men and women and that life satisfaction often increases with the departure of the last child from the home (Gass, 1959; Glenn, 1975; Lowenthal and Chiriboga, 1972). In contrast, Bart (1967) found that depressed mid-life women suffered a loss of self-esteem from the empty nest. "Probably one of the most serious problems confronting married women is that of finding something meaningful to do after their children grow up" (Gove, 1972, p. 35). When mid-life couples were asked to compare the empty-nest period with earlier periods in their lives, more wives than husbands evaluated the postparental time both more positively and less positively (Deutscher, 1964). In other words, the postparental time was more marked one way or the other for the women than for the men.

Sontag (1972) and Winn and Daly (1971) observed that, for many women, youthful physical attractiveness becomes a necessity for the maintenance of self-esteem. Nowak and Troll (1974) agreed that attractiveness is important for the self-concept of women in the middle years, but they distinguished youthfulness from attractiveness. They examined six age groups of women to determine concern with attractiveness and youthfulness at different ages. Women between thirty-five and fifty-four were more concerned with attractiveness than both the younger and older groups. The greatest preoccupation with attractiveness was noted among those around age fifty. Women's concern with youthfulness increases across the life span, with a noticeable plateau occurring between ages thirty-five and fifty-four. Nowak and Troll (1974) speculated that this plateau might be a result of the empty-nest period, which allows mid-life women to resume youthful activities that they did not have time to enjoy during their mothering years.

Whatever the motivations for the return of these women to school, supportive social networks composed of family and friends are extremely important to them. Disruptions in these support systems become critical when husbands are displeased with their wives' departure for the classroom. Women in this situation report far greater stress in adjusting to the requirements of study. Again, other studies suggest that aging brings gender-specific changes that can exacerbate this problem. For example, the affiliative and companionship needs of the husband tend to increase, while the assertive needs of the wife become more pronounced (Gruenbaum, 1979).

Returning women students who enroll in educational programs need to manage different life tasks than their younger counterparts do. They are not dealing with the type of emotional turmoil that most young people experience as they first set out to live apart from their parents. They are not involved in the social rituals that accompany mate selection, at least not for the first time. Most are not learning to handle budgets, manage housekeeping, or clarify their values. But, unlike the younger students, they bring with them the problems and challenges of balancing family demands with study, concerns for the health of older parents, and stress resulting from feelings that this education is a last-chance opportunity. They cannot be cavalier about failure.

Adding and Adjusting Programs and Services

Clearly, the needs and experiences of older women students are sufficiently unlike those of younger cohorts to justify development of new programs and adjustment of existing programs. To suggest this, however, is not to imply that older students need or want to be segregated from younger students. It is to say that there is strong evidence that they need programs and services unique to their needs (for example, physical health programs or programs that assess learning from life and work experience), and that what is already available may need some modification (for example, scheduling of classes or hours of operation for such facilities as bookstores and libraries). Where institutions find themselves competing for students with other institutions, those who try to meet the special requirements of older students will find themselves better prepared to compensate for the declining enrollment among younger students.

To illustrate what an institution can do to facilitate the return of mature women, I will describe the University of Georgia's Women's Opportunities Network (WON) in detail.

The Women's Opportunities Network

WON is a volunteer group of fifteen faculty, staff, and student women who joined together in 1979 to examine and begin to address the problems and needs of nontraditional women students on their campus. Network women represent various facets of campus life, such as student activities, counseling and testing, health services, housing, continuing education, academic affairs, and evening classes. Several members have themselves experienced interruption of an educational program by major life events (such as marriage, children, divorce, widowhood), and they can identify with women who have found it necessary to delay their academic pursuits. Because of the commitment, experience, and resources of these network women, re-entry women students have access to a support system that is available on a large university campus.

One of the most difficult tasks for any organization is the formulation of goals and objectives. After much deliberation, the members of WON agreed on four goals: to promote and facilitate the development of services, activities, and programs for the growth and development of mature women students in areas of their special interests and needs; to advise the university administration on the concerns of mature women students; to maintain a program of research on the older-than-average university student; and to serve as an advocate and resource for mature women students in their total educational experience. They also agreed on four objectives: to incorporate orientation into the existing program of the admissions office; to suggest inserts related to the needs and interests of older students for the existing handbook; to re-examine all findings from surveys, computer data, orientation, and so forth, to begin preparing information for deans, department heads, faculty, and any others who could benefit from access to this information; and to develop a faculty in-service program based on these findings.

Although many may think these goals and objectives simple and easily attainable, those who have experience with any support group—whether for women, minorities, or international students—realize the difficulties involved in their actual realization.

One early and major undertaking of the Network was a survey by mail of 1,600 women students between the ages of twenty-six and seventy-eight. The survey compiled demographic information on these students and determined specific needs and problems that they had encountered on campus. The six most reported problems that these women identified were demands on their time and energy, financial concerns, finding time to study, keeping up with family responsibilities, parking on the campus, and keeping up with their social life.

The women wanted the university to provide six kinds of service: health and gynecological services, career and vocational counseling, personal counseling, women's support groups, a women's center, and periodic social activities for older students. Asked to identify programs that they would like to attend, they named such topics as legal rights, equal rights, managerial skills for women, and exercise and weight control.

Open-ended responses provided additional insights about their needs and situations. The women surveyed wanted the faculty to be more sensitive to adult students. They wanted childcare facilities for student parents, campus and library orientations, opportunities to take entire degree programs in evening school. They wanted the bookstore to stay open at least two nights a week, and they wanted more courses scheduled in the late afternoon.

These findings are in keeping with the findings of many other surveys. For example, Smallwood (1980) found that the three most pressing problems for re-entry women were coordinating studies with childcare and family responsibilities, coordinating studies with jobs and time constraints, and knowing how to study efficiently.

Since WON was formed in 1979, several new activities and projects have been conducted. A reception and orientation for re-entry women students introduced them to some existing campus services and to the members of WON, who discussed their personal experiences in higher education and conveyed their sense of commitment to these women. Later, WON sponsored a program to present the results of the survey just described to these women and others from the campus community who were interested in its findings.

The major event sponsored by WON was an orientation program for the re-entry woman in fall 1980. It was prepared with special attention to the needs identified in the survey and with the intention that it would become an annual event. Three goals were established for the orientation:

to assist mature women in their transition to campus life, to enable participants to meet other students in similar situations, and to acquaint participants with the people on the campus who managed services and programs designed to meet their needs.

Forty-four women attended the event. The evaluations indeed attested to the fact that the goals were achieved. Women were pleased with the informality, the information provided, the opportunity to meet others like themselves, the capability of the panel, and the empathy and understanding evidenced. When asked how they felt they could be assisted in their return, they recommended listening to their concerns, helping with career counseling, and providing network support.

Besides pursuing its own efforts to reach re-entry women, WON has been the catalyst for a variety of spin-off programs for mature students on campus. A Nontraditional Student Group (NTSG) has been formed; a continuing education program for adults who are "contemplating" entering or re-entering the university has been developed; several health programs on such topics as diet, exercise, and depression have been initiated; and luncheons to acquaint university faculty women with the goals and objectives of WON have been held.

As the Women's Opportunities Network entered its third year of semiofficial existence on campus, the membership was asked what concrete influences the organizaton had had. The most specific influence mentioned was creation of the Division of Student Affairs' Adult Student Services Committee in 1981. The committee was composed of representatives from nine university areas. Five representatives were members of WON. For the first year, the committee's charge was fourfold: to assess the needs of older, nontraditional, and part-time students; to coordinate services for adult learners; to focus on ways in which university departments and agencies can become both aware of and responsive to the needs of older students; and to provide written recommendations to the associate vice-president for student affairs regarding needs of and services for this emerging student population. The members of WON felt that they had accomplished a major portion of their mission with the establishment of this committee. They were delighted to learn that it was to assume future responsibility for the orientation of adult students.

Other examples of WON's influence on the University of Georgia campus are occasional luncheons with women faculty across the campus, thereby increasing the visibility both of adult students and of the network system; study skills programs for evening students; adult student coffees funded by university evening classes; revision of student affairs publications to include information pertinent to returning women, counseling workshops tailored for returning women, designation of certain counselors in student affairs offices to work with returning students, development of a network of women faculty in the College of Education, and heightened sensitivity to adult students in academic advising in the College of Arts and Sciences. Some might argue that all these activities could have occurred despite the formation of WON and the stimulation that it provided. Yet, there is rather clear evidence that the organization has raised the campus consciousness regarding older students.

One member of WON stated, "I think the informal network is the single most valuable resource I use in my counseling. Many people call me for very unusual reasons (medical advice, geographical advice, nursery school information, and so forth) since I am advertised in the independent study brochure as Adult Advisory Service. If it were not for WON network, I would have to be the cold, impersonal voice on the phone to these people, not a human being who can sometimes help. The network enables me to untangle the unnecessary red tape of the university. I still think that humanism and concern are possible in the midst of a large university. The humanism of WON makes my job work for students in ways that would not otherwise be possible. I don't see WON changing the university in earth-shattering ways, but I see the ties changing individual lives in significant ways."

Other Programs and Resources for Returning Women Students. One successful and innovative project has demonstrated the value of volunteer work for re-entry into the labor force. In partnership with ten potential employers in Boston, the directors of the Women's Career Project at Northeastern University in Boston developed a pilot program that identified managerial and technical aspects of available positions and the skills necessary for performance of those jobs. Project directors noted that recruitment too often has focused on degree credentials and previous paid work experience. Thus, three considerations were emphasized in the design of this project: First, many women wishing to turn to careers have already acquired competencies, through unpaid work, that are transferable to the world of work. Second, traditional degree programs are not only too long and too costly but often irrelevant to the work objectives of these women. Third, traditional hiring practices do not recognize or credit unpaid work. Through conferences, where women were assisted in skill identification, and sensitive and appropriate course development, project participants were trained to enter into employment. One especially meaningful facet of this project was that these women's volunteer and unpaid community experiences could be transferred to paid work positions.

In New Haven, Connecticut, a program called New Careers for Women was begun by Yale faculty wives, although the program is not directly affiliated with any institution. New Careers provides career guidance, business skills training, and a five-month managerial internship in a nearby business or service agency. The internship is conducted without pay to the student. Business and agencies that offer the internships are expected to provide references to potential employers on the student's performance and ability. As with the Women's Career Project at Northeastern, experience on the job is emphasized, and academic degrees are inconsequential.

In a nine-month business course, Management Development for Women, at Fairfield University, students neither receive diplomas nor job guarantees. The developers and managers of this program work closely with nearby business and industry to tailor courses that meet their needs. They are aided in this by an advisory board that represents large corporations in that geographical area.

Educational Testing Service of Princeton, New Jersey, has conducted and prepared some excellent materials on the awarding of academic credit for homemaking skills and volunteer participation. Three of their workbooks are *How to Get College Credit for What You Have Learned as a Homemaker and Volunteer, Evaluating Women's Life Experience Competencies for College and Credit,* and *Volunteer Work and College Credit.*

Another extraordinary program is the Continuing Education for Women program at the University of Michigan. Heavily supported by the Ford Foundation, the program is recognized for the assistance that it offers to women who want counseling and guidance related to re-entry in college degree programs. Among the valuable resources prepared by Center librarians is a "Women's Life Cycle and Public Policy Conference Bibliography."

Old Dominion University's Women's Center in Norfolk has operated for several years. The conferences offered through this center have frequently attracted national participation.

Use of a continuing education program as a transition aid for adult women returning to college is exemplified by Seminar College: An Academic Interlude, a program of the University of Michigan's Detroit Extension Center. This experimental noncredit program for women who have not been involved in higher education or the labor force for a considerable time enables women to become reacquainted with academic pursuits without the demands and requirements of a graded experience.

Second Wind: A Program for Returning Women Students, a program developed by the Counseling Center of the University of Maryland at College Park, illustrates the "Each one teach one" strategy that has been applied on many campuses. That is, the first generation of returning women trained under this program assumed leadership responsibilities for assisting others like themselves with the challenges of re-entry. Training included an overview of the entire program. Areas emphasized were educational skills development, career advisement, minority education, orientation, teaching aide, and workshop leader.

Lessons Learned

Despite the increased availability of programs, an older woman must make many considerations when she contemplates returning to school. The following checklist (see Figure 1) was prepared from WON surveys of nontraditional women. It demonstrates some factors that older women might need to consider before seeking college admission:

Figure 1. A Checklist for Re-entry and Nontraditional Women Students

---

Does the institution that you are thinking about entering give consideration to the following six instructional and service areas: institutional commitment, curriculum, information services, social support services, financial aid, and logistics?

Institutional Commitment

_____ Are the faculty sensitized to older students; that is, do they appreciate and realize that part-time and full-time women students most often are extremely serious? In other words, do they recognize the adult status of these students?

Information Services

_____ Is there a special campus orientation for nontraditional students?
_____ Is there a library orientation for older students?

Social Support Services

_____ Are services provided to help older students with research paper writing and other study skills? Is tutoring provided?
_____ Are there women's groups on the campus, both for general support and for examining special issues, such as assertiveness and sexual harassment?
_____ Is there a women's center or meeting place, with lockers, a bulletin board, and a cooking area for commuters?
_____ Are there professionals on the campus who can provide help with decision making for careers and career planning?
_____ What types of social activities are planned for students older than twenty-two? Are there social activities for families?
_____ Is there housing on the campus especially suitable for older students?
_____ Is there a career placement office where nontraditional students are assisted in finding employment or with such matters as job interviewing techniques?
_____ Are there counseling and testing services that recognize the needs and concerns of nontraditional students? Are these services available in the evenings?

Financial Aid

_____ Are there work study opportunities for older students?
_____ Does the institution provide special opportunities for its employees to take courses?
_____ Are older students aware of financial aid and loans? Are there staff on the campus prepared to help nontraditional students seeking financial services?

Logistics

_____ Is it possible to take all the courses that one needs for a degree or certificate by attending evening classes? Are there weekend courses?

_____ Are courses scheduled by the institution to take into consideration the life-styles of nontraditional students?

_____ Are child care services available on campus? Do these services provide the type of child care that can assist while a parent attends a few classes? Is child care available in the evenings? Is there a mothers' cooperative?

_____ Is there ample parking on the campus at all times?

_____ Is the bookstore open in the evenings or late afternoons? Is the bookstore open on the weekends?

Curriculum

_____ Is there a women's studies program on the campus?

_____ Is it possible to get academic credit for learning from certain life experiences?

Institutional Commitment

_____ Is there a newsletter for nontraditional students or a telephone help line with information about campus programs, projects, and services?

There is probably no single institution in the United States that provides all the services suggested by this checklist. However, many of these services can be extremely important, perhaps essential, to returning women students. Further, checklist items illustrate programs and services that can be created or adjusted by institutions that are concerned with better meeting the needs of this clientele.

Conclusions

On many campuses the question still arises: Why design programs specifically for women? Are males who return to higher education not concerned about the same issues? It is important, especially in times of financial strain in higher education, to clarify what women's programs are and why they are necessary. The first category of women's programs deals with biological and psychological subjects, such as menopause, mother-daughter relationships, and sexual harassment. The second category includes programs that reflect the changing role of women in society, such as math anxiety among women, women in management, and women in politics. The third category includes programs, traditionally for men, that have recently become attractive to women, such as estate planning, automobile mechanics, and building investments. These three categories of women's programs are needed because they are biologically or psychologically of concern to females, because they deal with issues historically eliminated from women's learning experiences and life aspirations, or because they concern subjects that women have not been encouraged to pursue.

All these programs assist women with career transitions, especially when the transitions are into areas that have not generally been open to them. The important thing about these programs is that they examine issues that have historically been viewed predominantly from the male perspective from a woman's point of view. For example, a program on financial credit or a program on the different treatment of the sexes under law could vary considerably, depending on the sex and life experiences of the students; a single-sex program, in this case, could be the best way to approach the subject matter.

It is possible that, in years to come, women's programs will not need to be separated from other programs on such topics as legal status and financial credit; however, since the societal changes that will make the separate programs unnecessary seem to be slow in coming, programs designed specifically for women in higher education will remain important to the foreseeable future. Re-entry women will continue to seek programs that they perceive to carry the promise of career opportunities upon program completion. The message to institutions, then, is loud and clear: If institutions are interested in attracting women students to campus, they must create nontraditional programs that demonstrate an understanding of women's life cycle issues and needs.

Although projects, programs, and centers that serve returning women students abound, many colleges and universities still make no personnel or financial commitment to serving this clientele. The significance of a voluntary network like WON is magnified when it is the sole special resource that these women have. The larger the college or universities, the more essential such a network becomes. When a student tapes into the network at one point, she is automatically linked to many other people, as the interconnectedness of the members expands the information base for all who participate. Individually, none of the members has the resources or time to devote to individual tasks and problems that can be handled by the total network group. The very existence of a committed group of individuals who continue to update one another on issues and aids for adult women students sends a message to everyone on campus: a message to administrators that there is a need to serve older returning students, a message to faculty that these students often enter with a higher level of commitment to learning than traditional students have, a message to older students that their concerns are important and worthy to address, and a message to one another that a network is an efficient and exhilarating mechanism for binding resources and energies in novel and useful ways.

References

Aslanian, C. B., and Brickell, H. M. *Americans in Transition: Life Changes as Reasons for Adult Learning.* New York: College Entrance Examination Board, 1980.

Bart, P. B. "Depression in Middle-Aged Women: Some Sociocultural Factors." Unpublished doctoral dissertation, University of California, 1967.

Cytrynbaum, S., Blum, L., Patrick, R., Stein, J., Wadner, D., Wilk, C. "Midlife Development: A Personality and Social Systems Perspective." January 19, 1980 draft of a work scheduled to appear in L. Poon (Ed.) *Aging in the 1980s: Selected Contemporary Issues in the Psychology of Aging.* Washington, D.C.: American Psychological Assn., 1980.

Deutscher, I. "Quality of Post Parental Life: Definitions of the Situation." *Journal of Marriage and the Family,* 1964, *26* (1), 52–59.

Gass, G. Z. "Counseling Implications of Women's Changing Role." *Personnel and Guidance Journal,* 1959, *37* (7), 486.

Glenn, N. D. "Psychological Well-Being in the Postparental Stage: Some Evidence from National Surveys." *Journal of Marriage and the Family,* 1975, *37* (1), 105–110.

Gove, W. R. "The Relationship Between Sex Roles, Marital Status, and Mental Illness." *Social Forces,* 1972, *51* (1), 34–44.

Gruenbaum, H. "Middle Age and Marriage: Affiliative Men and Assertive Women." *American Journal of Family Therapy,* 1979, *7* (3), 46–50.

Gutmann, D., Grunes, J., and Griffin, B. *Transitions of Aging.* New York: Academic Press, 1980.

Lowenthal, M. F., and Chiriboga, D. "Transition to the Empty Nest: Crisis, Challenge, or Relief?" *Archives of General Psychiatry,* 1972, *26* (2), 8–14.

Margolis, D. R. "A Fair Return? Back to College at Middle Age." *Change,* 1974, *6* (8), 34–37.

Nowak, C. A., and Troll, L. E. "Age Concept on Women: Concern with Youthfulness and Attractiveness Related to Self-Perceived Age." Paper presented at the 27th annual meeting of the Gerontological Society, Portland, Ore., 1974.

Smallwood, K. B. "What Do Adult Women College Students Really Need?" *Journal of College Student Personnel,* 1980, *21* (1), 65–73.

Sontag, S. "The Double Standard of Aging." *Saturday Review,* 1972, *55* (39), 29–38.

Winn, H. D., and Daly, J. J. "The Changes of Life in Woman." *Geriatrics,* 1971, *26* (6), 105–111.

Margaret Holt is an assistant professor in the Adult Education Department at the University of Georgia and an assistant to the dean of the College of Education. Since July 1981, she has represented the University of Georgia in a national project to develop a national Domestic Policy Association. Her most recent publication "Strategies for the 'Ascent of Woman' in Higher Education Administration in the 1980s," appeared in the Journal of the National Association of Women Deans, Administrators, and Counselors.

*The truly effective physician, attorney, and
psychologist all know more than medicine, law, and
psychology. They have learned about themselves as
adults in transition and as practicing professionals.
Can professional schools address these issues of professional socialization and adult development?*

Professional Socialization
and Adult Development
in Graduate
Professional Education

David L. Singer

I grew up in Brooklyn. My father, a small-town lawyer in a big city, was
and still is a highly rational and deeply idealistic man. He sometimes has
a difficult time seeing people and the world as they really are, I think. My
mother left teaching when I was less than a year old to devote full time to
raising a family. She returned to that profession some fifteen years later,
loved her work, and until her retirement probably earned from her teaching as much as my father did from his law practice. While she was never
great at logical argument and seldom clear about the names of public
figures or about current events (much to my father's consternation), she
could always see people and events with a keenly realistic eye and always
seemed to understand what made them tick.

Earlier versions of this chapter were presented at the January 1981 meetings
of the American Association of Law Schools in San Antonio, Texas, and at the
May 1981 Workshop on Supervision of the Antioch New England Graduate
School.

B. Menson (Ed.). *New Directions for Experiential Learning: Building on
Experiences in Adult Development*, no. 16. San Francisco: Jossey-Bass, June 1982.

An older cousin of mine entered graduate school in clinical psychology when I was about ten years old. From then on, every few years my mother would say, "Have you ever thought about going into psychology? It is a good profession. Look at Jerome." However, I intended to be a lawyer, like my father.

As a child, I tried very hard to be smart and to be "right." I went to Brooklyn College, then to the Yale Law School. There, I spent an exciting, even mind-boggling, year learning about the differences between the Brooklyn Jewish culture and the Yale culture. Years later, I heard rumors that the "Yale way" was to "dress British, think Yiddish," but if it was like that when I was there, I certainly did not know it (or I couldn't have heard it if someone told me). I also learned something about the law, and I learned less than something about the realities of lawyering. Perhaps most important of all, during that year at the Yale Law School, I married a woman who was a graduate student in the Yale psychology department. I found that I preferred the way in which psychologists view the world to the way in which lawyers view the world, and I learned that I did not need to follow in my father's footsteps to please either him or myself. So, I switched to graduate study in clinical psychology.

My career as a psychology graduate student was not smooth. I found that I had to trade my lawyer's style of judging for the psychologist's way of understanding. Along the way, my first marriage ended. I had to give up the previously unconscious fantasy that I as a therapist would sit in judgment on others and thus escape their sitting in judgment on me. I also had to learn to receive supervision and mentorship from faculty and senior colleagues. Four years of personal psychoanalysis certainly helped in this process.

During my last year in graduate school, at age twenty-six, I taught a course in child psychology at a local college to finance the trip to Europe that I had promised myself after completing my dissertation. In so doing, I once again confronted (and this time to become better friends with) the child in me, and I came to the realization that, despite my clinical training with adults, I could not fully understand them without fully understanding the child in them. As a result, I decided to take a year of postdoctoral training in clinical work with children.

While the preceding paragraphs could seem like a digression into personal material that might better be left for consideration between myself and some analyst or with a good friend over drinks at the end of the day, I suggest that they are directly relevant to the topic at hand. You see, I think my history is rather more typical than less typical, in that my experience of professional training was inextricably bound up with my own adult development, which was itself interwoven with themes and residues from my earlier life. Most professionals, I suggest, would have a similar story to tell. My experience as a clinician and teacher bears this out, and certainly this is one of the main themes that emerges from life history research on adult development (Levinson and others, 1978).

This leads directly to the topic that I will address here: the interface and interpenetration among the tasks of professional education, the psychology and adult development of students, and the structures and processes (both formal and informal) of professional training programs. Over the past several years, we in the Department of Professional Psychology at the Antioch New England Graduate School have evolved a point of view about professional education that has led us to conceptualize and design our programs in some rather unique ways. In this chapter, I shall first describe the general perspective that we have developed about professional training. Next, I will describe how we have used this point of view to develop an approach to graduate education in professional psychology that has already been carried out in our masters programs and that will also inform a doctoral program that begins in summer 1982.

A Theoretical Perspective

Our perspective on professional education focuses on two interrelated elements: the task of professional education and the issues facing students. On the first element, we view the task of professional education as preparation for effective role functioning. On the second, we are impressed by the importance of the facts that joining a profession invariably involves a socialization process, which profoundly affects students' lives; that this process takes place in the context of students' adult development and in the light of students' experience of self as they essay various roles involved in being both a student and a fledgling member of the field; and that both joining a profession and attending professional school are highly stressful experiences for most students.

These perspectives have led us to a view of the process of professional education. We believe that an effective program in professional psychology needs to provide vehicles through which students can share and collectively explore their experiences in the various roles involved in being student professionals. Thus far, our experience is that this opportunity considerably enhances the overall impact of the program, with little or no sacrifice in students' effective theoretical and conceptual preparation or skill development.

The Task of Professional Education. If we define professional education as preparation for effective role functioning, several things follow. First, professional education then encompasses not only teaching the substantive knowledge and theory in the field and the technical skills involved in their application, but it also involves working with students so that they become aware of the different ways in which they can take up the profession and use their training to forge an initial career. Law students, for example, need to decide whether to pursue an initial career as corporate counsel; as a public interest attorney; as a member of a private firm in general or specialized practice; in policy development and planning with public or private agencies; in mediation, arbitration, and adjudication; in administration; or in teaching and scholarship. Psychologists in training must address similar choices. Do they wish to be clinicians in the public or private sector? To work with individuals or with families; in industry, with schools, or in the mental health system; as consultant educators, as direct service deliverers, or as program developers and administrators?

Certain activities, roles, and relationships are associated with each of these ways of being a member of one's chosen profession. Each requires different sets of personal as well as technical skills, and each has its own set of dynamics, demands, and strains. Exploring these different ways of being a professional—especially through practical experience—seems to us to be a necessary part of professional education. It provides students with opportunities to taste their own reactions to various activities, roles, situations, and relationships and to find out what parts of the self are evoked. Inevitably, they begin to gravitate towards some activities, roles, and relationships and to avoid others; they begin to resolve tensions evoked by activities, roles, and relationships that stir up conflicting feelings, and they tap unresolved personal issues. A professional school not only can but should guide and facilitate this process. To do so, we have found, involves attending to the role and personal issues that students encounter as they go through the process of professional education. Yet, very little in the literature on the process of professional socialization acknowledges or addresses these issues (Bucher and Stelling, 1977). Let us examine three of these issues: those having to do with the self, adult development, and stress in graduate school.

Professional Socialization and the Self. Joining a profession is a complex process, which involves much more than the acquisition of concepts, information, and skills. It involves joining a culture which has its own values, norms, and language (Clark, 1973). One's profession tends to get inside of one's self and become a part of one's identity. One learns to think as psychologists, physicians, or lawyers do; to see the world from the perspective of one's discipline; to feel akin to others in the field; and to function in the various roles that fall to members of one's chosen field. Perhaps most importantly, if one is to survive and flourish, one must be able to do all this in a way that is consonant with the valued parts of one's self without stretching the limits of what seems acceptable to other members of the profession.

The integration of self with the various activities and roles involved in one's chosen field is a complex matter in any profession and at any age. Each field has its own unique dilemmas and others that it shares with allied professions. Physicians, for example, must learn early how to manage relationships with people who regard them as magical or god-like, with people who are terrified and who look to them for salvation from mysterious, invasive, and overpowering forces that threaten their body, if not their very life. This involves learning to handle not only the fears and dependency of others but the parallel issues in themselves, as well as their own reactions to mortality, disfigurement, and death. How they resolve these issues will either enhance or detract from their effectiveness with patients, and it will either enhance or detract from their own emotional health and work satisfaction. As persons given large areas of responsibility, they must also learn to manage relationships with subordinates and coprofessionals and to negotiate the complex power relationships within hospitals, clinics, and the medical community.

Lawyers' clients are often in a state of hostile dependency—feeling a desperate need for help yet resenting the person or group to whom they must go. Young attorneys, while doubting their own abilities, as do fledgling members of any profession, must learn to differentiate between their own needs and problems and those of their clients—between what is "inside" and what is "outside" if they are to be effective. The attorney recovering from a personal marital separation who acts out resentment towards an abandoning spouse by being abusive to witnesses in divorce and custody cases, by pushing for unreasonably punitive settlements against members of the opposite sex, or by not being empathic and by poorly advising or representing a client of the opposite sex, is hardly functioning competently. As many authors have highlighted (Stone, 1971; Watson, 1968), the adversarial nature of much legal work provides a special challenge to young lawyers, given their own aggressive impulses, hostility, competitiveness, and need to be loved. Maintaining adequate personal distance from the combative elements of the work without losing one's sensitivity to the emotional nuances of complicated situations is no easy matter. Nevertheless, learning to understand and inspire confidence in clients is critical in bringing business to the law firm; indeed, this, more than any other factor, determines success in private legal practice, I am told.

Working with dependency and distress pose similar dilemmas to psychologists in their role as therapist. If they are to serve their clients well and not act out their own unmet needs and unresolved issues on their clients, they must come to grips with their own problems, their own fears, and their own concerns about loss of control. In their roles as managers or clinic unit heads, they need to deal with the dilemmas involved in representing various groups and interests and in occupying positions of institutional authority. As researchers and program evaluators, they must deal with others who may fear being criticized or proved ineffective; this means coming to terms with their own issues surrounding evaluation, intrusion, and approval.

In my experience, most programs of professional training in most disciplines do an adequate job of training students in the conceptual bases of the profession and in helping students to think and see the world in a way that is both consonant with and useful for members of their profession. However, most programs do a much poorer job in helping students to understand and learn to function in the variety of roles that face the professional in real life and they do very little to help students to identify and address the personal dilemmas attendant on joining the field.

Adult Development. Professional socialization and the integration of self with one's new profession takes place in the context of the student's adult development. Our awareness of adult development and its significance is relatively new. Although certain writers, such as Erik Erikson, have attempted to draw our attention to this phenomenon for years, until recently the prevailing wisdom was that development took place up until age twenty or so. This was followed by a long plateau called adulthood, which in turn was followed by a slow, steady decline. Thanks to the work of Daniel Levinson and his colleagues (Levinson and others, 1978), Roger Gould (1972, 1978), and others, we now have come to understand that the development of the self, its capacities, and the life structure—the patterning of self in the world—are ongoing processes that take place throughout the entire life cycle.

As educators involved in professional training of adult learners, we have found this line of theory and research to be rich in implications for understanding the meaning of returning to school in adulthood and for thinking about the meaning of work and career at different stages of the life cycle. It provides guideposts that identify some of the typical dilemmas and tasks of each stage of the adult life cycle and some of the childhood myths (Gould, 1978) that must be shed at each juncture along the way.

Levinson's group (Levinson and others, 1978) has found that there are alternating periods of stability and transition in the life cycle for men, with major transitional periods occurring more or less around the turn of decades (that is, between age seventeen and twenty-two, twenty-eight and thirty-two, thirty-eight and forty-two, and so on), with some rather amazing consistencies. Each stable period and each transitional period appear to have their own particular tasks and their own normative phenomena, issues, and dilemmas. Wendy Stewart (1976) has corroborated the cyclical nature of the life cycle for women. She found that transitional periods tend to occur more or less at the decades for women as well, although the content and dilemmas of each period tend to differ somewhat from those of men.

The model graduate student in our department is a woman around thirty years of age. Many students enter in their mid to late twenties, while others begin graduate study in their mid thirties or even later. As we interview them at entry and observe their struggles and progress in becoming professional psychologists, we are struck by how real the differences are between students at different stages of adult development.

The student in the mid twenties is, in Levinson's framework (Levinson and others, 1978), entering the adult world—taking tentative steps towards making commitments to a stable life structure while at the same time remaining distant enough to maintain an experimental posture and to preclude becoming prematurely locked in a life structure that does not fit well. As one might imagine, students in their twenties often experience crises of commitment and have periods of extreme doubt about psychology as the right field for them. Often, they make us wonder as well. During this period, students are attempting to find ways of living out what Levinson calls "the dream."

The dream is somewhat more than a fantasy and somewhat less than a fully formed plan; it begins as a vague sense of the self in the adult world. As Levinson (Levinson and others, 1978, p. 91) put it, "It has the quality of a vision and imagined possibility that generates excitement and vitality. At the start, it is poorly articulated and only tenuously connected to reality, although it may contain concrete images, such as winning the Nobel Prize or making the all-star team." For most aspiring professionals, the dream contains imagery involving the world of work and how one will relate to the economic and social order. But, whatever the nature of the dream, the task at hand is to find ways of giving it greater definition and living it out.

During this period students also frequently enter into mentoring relationships. As described by Levinson (Levinson and others, 1978), the mentor relationship is special and complex—a sort of love relationship with someone, neither parent nor peer, who is both in some mixture. The mentor's special function is to sponsor, guide, and host the young adult, typically in the occupational world. Mentors are usually half a generation older; often they are a teacher, boss, or senior colleague. The mentor's primary function is to support and facilitate realization of the dream. Mentoring relationships are usually transitional, often intense, and often short-lived, but they are always long-remembered, and the mentor becomes an important figure in the inner world of the developing adult.

Both the dream and the mentor are connected to the process of forming an occupation. This typically begins with initial choice of an occupation in the early twenties and continues to be an active (if not difficult) process throughout the first half of early adulthood, typically reaching completion only after the transition at age thirty. Sometimes, the process is linear; sometimes it is more complex, with the young person struggling to sort out multiple interests and identifications with important people from the personal and mythic past and to find ways of living out the important and valued part of the self in the world of work.

Forming love relationships, marriage, and family is a key developmental task of early adulthood. This task, too, is very complex, with many residues from preadulthood needing to be worked out in the process. This process is often linked to the dream and to forming an occupation, with the excitement and appeal of potential partners either enhanced or diminished by the degree to which they show promise for filling a role in the dream and the vision of occupation within it. At times, the demands of occupation and love relationships conflict, and there is consequent stress in both domains.

Throughout this period of the late twenties, students are also grappling with having to relinquish some of the false assumptions that have guided them thus far. Especially in psychology, they must give up the notion that there is one right way to be, to live, to feel, or to do things. Often, they find that marriage or a relationship with the "special" man or woman cannot achieve for them what they cannot achieve for themselves. All of this is both painful and conducive to growth, and it flavors both their professional work and their functioning as students.

Professional schools have a unique potential and responsibility to assist young adults in the process of forming an occupation for themselves. First, they may help students to explore what they are hoping (consciously or otherwise) to find in their chosen profession and whether this is indeed realistic for them. Are they living out some family romance, an unfulfilled ambition of one parent or the other? Are they compensating for an old wound? Second, by providing reality checks, professional schools can provide both support for the occupational aspects of a young person's dream and opportunities to forestall subsequent disillusionment. The idealized occupation can be compared with the opportunities as they really exist. Third, professional schools can foster students' professional development by providing opportunities from which mentoring relationships can emerge, either with faculty or with senior members of the profession.

What of students who begin graduate or professional school a bit later? The student who enters graduate or professional school in the late twenties or early thirties is likely to be in the midst of, or terminating the age thirty transition described for men by Levinson and colleagues (Levinson and others, 1978) and for women by Stewart (1976). For both sexes, this is a period of profound reassessment of the early adult life structure, and it is often quite painful. Gould suggests that this is a period during which the major false assumption to be reassessed is that "Life is simple and controllable. There are no significant coexisting contradictory forces within me" (1978, p. 153). Beginning to acknowledge the limitations of purely intellectual knowledge, the unwanted parts of one's parents in oneself, the complexity and primitive quality of intimate relationships, and the fragility of seemingly secure relationships and life structures are all part of this process, according to Gould. Our students in this age group bear this out. It is a time of mellowing and of the emergence of wisdom, as contrasted with the brightness of younger students.

For men, the age thirty transition typically represents an effort to bring one's life into greater congruence with one's dream and one's newly emerging awareness and to better live out the heretofore unexpressed parts of oneself. A return to graduate or professional school at this stage in life is likely to reflect a major decision, which is an outgrowth of and which is colored by the internal processes that take place around these issues. Women at the age thirty transition are typically grappling with integrating two basic aspects of the life structure: the need for development of the self as an individual and the need to develop relational aspects of the self. Women who earlier pursued a relational dream (marriage, children, and so forth) find themselves at the age thirty transition trying to create ways to develop their own competence and self as a professional person before it becomes too late and before they feel that their lives have become overly dominated by husbands, children, lovers, and parents. Needless to say, the woman who enters graduate or professional school in the midst of the age thirty transition has much sorting out to do, especially since research seems to show that making the final separation from one's mother is a key task of this period, and this task almost always involves great stress and emotional upheaval.

According to Levinson (Levinson and others, 1978) the mid thirties are structure-building years, a time when the now not so young adult strives to settle down into a community and occupational world and then, in the late thirties, to become a senior and respected member within them. In my own experience as a professional and graduate educator, students in their mid thirties do indeed appear less chaotic. Most who return to school at that time seem recently to have made major life decisions, and they appear to be implementing a new life structure, in part by pursuing advanced training.

Students around age forty, however, particularly men, appear to be grappling with what Levinson (Levinson and others, 1978) calls the midlife transition. They are concerned with issues of mortality and disillusionment (seeing life and the self as they really are, not as one fantasizes them to be). As Levinson describes it (Levinson and others, 1978) this period is characterized by attempts to reintegrate polarities of the self to male and female, destructive and creative, old and young, and attachment and separateness, to accept the complexity and irreconcilability of differing role demands, mortality and aging, and the accompanying sense of limits on the time left in one's professional life. In my experience with graduate education in professional psychology, men who seek to become psychotherapists at this juncture are in part using their training as a vehicle to facilitate their getting in touch with heretofore neglected aspects of the self—typically the nurturing, feeling, caring, and intuitive functions.

For each age group, then, the process of professional education has a different meaning, which infuses their participation in professional or graduate school and colors their experience of it. We, as professional educators of professionals, have both the opportunity and the responsibility to help each student to integrate her or his own developing self with what is possible within the world of her or his profession, acknowledging the differences at different ages and trying, where possible, to teach around these differences. How to do this—how to build this into the curriculum and process of professional education—is the challenge.

Stress. Both joining a profession and the process of professional education are experienced by many as inherently stressful, often as an assault upon their sense of self-esteem as well. This phenomenon is rather well documented. The stress exhibits itself in many forms: stress-related psychophysiological disorders ranging from headaches and loss of sleep, through eczema and ulcers, to colitis, accident proneness and suicide, relationship and marital distress, and family difficulties (Halleck, 1976).

Each profession has its own characteristic sources of stress, and students in each profession develop characteristic coping styles, which run the gamut from the effective to the counterproductive. The intense competitiveness and the Socratic method of teaching at law schools tend to produce what students of legal education have termed "character warp," which takes the form of suppressed emotion and competitive intellectualization on the one hand and of alienation and withdrawal from engagement with law school on the other (Stone, 1971; Watson, 1968). The huge responsibility for life and death, together with the grueling hours of study and clinical work, often lead the medical student, intern, and resident physician to become emotionally distant from patients and to block out their awareness of their emotional reactions and needs.

We in psychology have similar dilemmas, although the stress emanates less from the wellsprings of competitive pressure than from fears of inadequacy in the face of human despair in the consulting room and of madness in oneself and from the strain placed on pre-existing relationships as students learn to understand behavior in new ways. The defensive characterological outcomes that can emerge among psychologists—condescending diagnosis of everyone and anything in sight on the one hand and indiscriminate understanding and love for everyone and everything on the other—are neither more pleasant nor more productive than the outcomes experienced by other professionals.

Charles Seashore (1975) has catalogued some of the stresses that cut across professions. These common stresses lead entering students in professional programs to expend more energy on survival than on growth and students at all levels of most programs to expend far more energy in the program than they expect to. Seashore identifies possible underlying reasons for this phenomenon. One possible reason is that, while the student applied to the program as an individual, the student was actually enrolling spouse, children, parents, lovers, and friends in "a change program which would likely provoke a wild and motley set of weird and delightful but sometimes torturous assortment of experiences" (p. 3). According to Seashore, the student first experiences being "deskilled, incompetent, emotionally out of commission, or just plain confused," (p. 6) then psychologically takes on the program as surrogate parent, surrogate lover, and source of role models as the student goes through a mini life cycle with the program. This is followed by crises of involvement, acceptance, and separation. Idealization of and rebellion against the school and faculty are stations along the way for some students as they try to reconcile their image of the profession with their image of themselves and as they work through old issues around parental authority.

Whether and how this stress is acknowledged and addressed by the professional school will have a powerful bearing on the way in which the student takes up the profession, on the internalized representations and images that the student develops about the profession, and on the way in which the student relates to the profession and to others in it. Until recently, educators in the professions have been slow to acknowledge the reality of these sources of stress and their consequences. They have been equally slow in accepting the responsibility for addressing these stresses systematically in ways other than referring stressed individuals to the local counseling or mental health facility. Of late, several professional schools have introduced various types of support groups, where students can identify and explore these stresses together and develop ways of coping with them. Research suggests that the presence of a social support network in students' lives is indeed effective in moderating the negative effects of stress (Goplerud, 1980). Our experience at Antioch New England Graduate School bears that out.

Education in Professional Psychology at the Antioch New England Graduate School

Ours is a practitioner-oriented graduate department whose students are adult learners living in a dispersed geographical region. Students drive up to two and one-half hours to attend one intensive day of classes on a year-round basis. During the rest of the week, they are either on half-time internships or practica. Some also work at jobs in psychology or another field to support themselves.

The faculty of the department have committed themselves to creating programs of professional preparation that sequence well-conceptualized and well-integrated courses both to promote the acquisition of a theory, concept, and skill base and to facilitate the professional socialization of students in a manner that is consonant with and enhanced by their personal styles and adult development.

Over the course of time, as we have refined our programs, our awareness of the issues thus far described indicates that the most effective professional preparation that we can offer our students consists of three elements: classroom experiences, in which concepts, theory, relevant empirical knowledge, and basic skills are provided; practical experiences—internships and practica in the workplace; and an integrative seminar, where an attempt is made to understand and integrate experience in the workplace not only with concepts, knowledge, and theory from the classroom but also with students' experience of self: their personal reactions, the transitions and seasons of their developing adult lives, and their emerging identities and conflicts as members of a profession.

We have also learned that an effective program of this kind must be more than a collection of isolated courses taught by individual experts. If it is to have any coherence as a socializing process that raises the self-awareness of students as developing professionals, a program must be planned and managed as an integrated sequence of experiences occurring within the context of a social system (a department, program, or school) that has a structure, social process, and culture, including a value system. These will inevitably influence the behavior of both faculty and students, and they will profoundly affect what the student takes away as the real learning. The program, department, or school must accept responsibility for the system that it creates and sustains. In addition, the faculty need to commit themselves to functioning as a work group, collectively pursuing a common task so that they each do an identified piece of the work on their own but clearly on behalf of the whole.

Such a perspective on professional education raises many dilemmas. It is hardly the traditional view of an academic institution. However, our experience thus far suggests that the process of professional training that I advocate here, when implemented in the model that I shall describe, can have several important beneficial effects on students: It helps them to cope with stress. It assists them in learning to identify and address tensions that exist for them in their professional roles and to find more creative, effective, and satisfying ways of engaging in professional activities. It sensitizes them to the difference between what is inside and outside of themselves so that they do not attempt to use colleagues or clients to solve personal conflicts or to meet personal needs. It heightens students' understanding and appreciation of theory and concepts as powerful tools in professional work. Finally, in some students, it results in a timely realization that they are misdirecting their energies and preparing for the wrong profession.

The Professional Seminar. A key vehicle for this process is called the *professional seminar.* Professional seminars contain between seven and ten students and one faculty person. Depending upon the students' program, they meet either two or two and one-half hours each week during the academic year. Students are members of a professional seminar for every year of their program. In the seminar, students explore together over time their experiences in their various roles as professionals in training, using their responses to each other's work and to behavior in the seminar as part of the material available to the group.

Professional seminar faculty lead seminar meetings, serve as academic advisor for seminar members, and make site visits to students' internship agencies. They are thus key faculty persons for seminar members, providing a critical link between the student and the program as well as between the program and the facilities in which students are interning or doing practicum work.

The professional seminar is a synthesized adaptation of several small-group educational techniques originally developed for use with adults in a variety of contexts. Techniques from which we have borrowed the most are the role relations seminar (Singer and Schachtel, 1981), the clinical supervision group (Rioch, Coulter, and Weinberger, 1976), and the theme-centered group as developed by Ruth Cohn (Schaffer and Galinsky, 1974).

The Role Relations Seminar. The role relations seminar is one component event of the group relations conferences developed at the Tavistock Institution in London during the 1960s, which are currently conducted in this country under the auspices of the A. K. Rice Institute and other educational organizations. These working conferences last between two and ten days. They provide participants with opportunities for in vivo study of behavior in groups and organizations through continual examination of ongoing events as they happen, in specially designed self-study exercises, with the aid of staff. One focus of these conferences is aspects of group and organizational behavior—often subtle and outside of conscious awareness—that center on authority issues, leader-follower relations, and collective management of anxiety. Specialized conferences have also been developed to address male-female relations, relations among persons at different stages of adult development, and among members of various professions. All these specialized conferences also focus on how different groups symbolize and stereotype themselves and others.

Role relations seminars toward the end of these conferences provide participants with an opportunity to discuss their experience in their various roles within the conference, to link these roles with concepts presented in lectures and assigned readings, and to apply their learnings in their roles at their real work settings. In much the same way, the professional seminar focuses on examination of experience and behavior at internship settings, Antioch, and home, using the "window" of one's role—what one was trying to accomplish, on whose behalf, and in what social system or organizational context; linking this with conceptual learnings from course work and readings; and systematically applying both learnings and experience to other situations and professional activities.

The Clinical Supervision Group. Individual clinical supervision is universally used as a primary training vehicle for mental health practitioners. It has the dual function of helping students to provide psychotherapeutic assistance to their clients and to grapple with the ways in which anxiety inherent in this type of work, their own life issues, and their own unresolved personal dilemmas can affect their therapeutic efforts. The supervisor typically functions more as an expert consultant than as a boss.

Group supervision is a more recent innovation. It has become widespread in recent years, not only because of its economy but also because, with effective leadership, it has unique potential. In particular, a cohesive group can provide the support, containment of anxiety, and protection of self-esteem that are necessary for pursuing this difficult work. The reactions of fellow students to the interactions between client and therapist serve as important material for everyone's learning. Group supervision can also offset, through numbers, the one-up one-down relationship inherent between supervisor and supervisee in individual supervision (Gustafson [1977] has described a variation of the supervision group for medical students, which he calls a seminar on "student doctor and patient relationships." This seminar, though case-focused, spends considerable time on the dilemmas experienced by developing physicians in their new role.

The Theme-Centered Group. This semistructured group technique was designed to help participants to cope more effectively with specific situations, transitions, or psychological issues, whether in the personal or professional parts of their lives. The theme-centered group is, for example, the method of choice in most quarters for consciousness-raising and support groups that help individuals to cope with a common adaptive dilemma, whether it be cancer, single parenthood, or loss of spouse. It has also become the predominant model for small-group discussion sessions at professional workshops for mental health and human service workers.

Three key features of the theme-centered group have been integrated in the professional seminar: conceptual input, personal experience, and examination of here-and-now interaction, that is, using what happens among participants in the group as material to explore for relevant learnings. Together, these features provide the tools with which professional seminars explore a content issue or an emerging general theme.

In the professional seminar, there is no predetermined curriculum or content in the traditional sense. Rather, given the basic overarching task, specific issues to be addressed are determined by student needs, interests, and experiences at their practicum or internship settings, in collaboration with the faculty member.

In practice, faculty have been successful in stimulating the development of an open and supportive culture, so that their professional seminars quickly become the students' "family group" at Antioch. Ethical, technical, and theoretical issues that emerge from students' work at their internship and practicum placements are discussed in depth. Professional seminars discuss how to use the power and "magic" inevitably invested by clients in the therapist in an ethical and responsible manner as well as the dynamics at work in their placement agency and their own role within the agency. They also spend at least some time each session with a case presentation or consultation with one of the members who has a crisis with a client to deal with. Perhaps most important, the professional seminar is a place where students can safely share and discuss the personal issues inevitably stimulated by clinical training—anxiety about one's own sanity and concern about one's adequacy and competency, to name only two—which serves to relieve much of the stress generated by carrying these concerns unexpressed, unexamined, and with the fantasy that "I am the only one who feels this way."

As a result of their unique role—seminar leader, academic advisor, and linkage with internship or practicum agency—professional seminar leaders are in a position to become aware of situations in which a student's personal issues are interfering with competent or ethical functioning, whether with clients, colleagues, or supervisors. This is a matter of serious concern, since we believe that we must be able to say that each of our graduates is fit for professional work. In such situations, the professional seminar provides a setting where such matters can be openly identified and where both the leader and other seminar members can engage the student in constructive work on them.

In order to help the faculty in carrying out their roles and to link each professional seminar with the program of which it is part, the five or six professional seminar leaders in each program meet together with the department's internship coordinator and their program coordinator biweekly for an hour. While these meetings serve a key student monitoring and administrative function within the department, they also enable us to keep our fingers in the emotional life of the department. Moreover, they are a professional seminar leaders' professional seminar. They provide support, peer consultation, and opportunity to share the dilemmas that professional seminar leaders experience in taking up their roles. Indeed, there is fairly strong agreement among faculty—all of whom are in clinical practice between one and four days a week as well as experienced teachers—that taking a professional seminar is the most personally demanding yet most rewarding teaching experience that they have known.

In summary, we believe that the successful professional seminar is a socialization vehicle that can help students in joining the internship and Antioch institutions and the profession and in leaving these institutions at the end of training while consolidating their newly found professional identity and while searching for a suitable role within the work world; a support group that facilitates the sharing of experiences with peers in a strengthening, growth-promoting way; an opportunity for understanding both their own adult development and the role of their career needs within it and in relation to it; a place in which students can integrate conceptual learning with practical experience gained from their internships and their life experience; opportunities to learn about and use the self as a tool for more effective functioning in professional roles; a forum for the discussion of ethical issues in psychology; and opportunities for developing mentoring relationships between faculty and students that enhance the growth and development of each.

Clearly, not all professional seminars succeed in all dimensions. However, a key test of any innovation in professional education lies in its impact on students: their satisfaction, their perception of the adequacy of their training, their ability to find positions upon graduation. By these standards, what we are doing appears to work. Through both informal discussions and formal alumni surveys, we find that increasing numbers of graduates are pleased with their training and securing jobs of the kind that they want. Although few are thoroughly familiar with the conceptual underpinnings of our educational approach, they all tend to pinpoint the professional seminar as a critical event in their training, one that differentiates it from their own previous educational experiences and even from those of friends and colleagues.

Conclusions

In this chapter, I have sought to communicate my excitement, both intellectual and personal, about what is happening in the Department of Professional Psychology of a small graduate school in rural New England. There, we are attempting to implement a view of education for professions that to our knowledge goes beyond what has been attempted elsewhere to date. Our view sees the task of professional education as one of helping the student—a whole person—to become a member of the profession: not only by learning the theory, knowledge, and techniques of the trade, but by examining and making sense of what it means to join *this* profession through *this* school at *this* stage of life under *this* set of life circumstances, using *this* internship experience, in a way that fits the student's sense of self. This view also claims that schools of professional training must organize themselves in special ways if they are to address professional training in this rich and full manner. A corollary of this view is that professional schools also need rich clinical opportunities as part of their program structure—the chance for students to function as members of their chosen profession in as near to real-life circumstances as is possible, so they have rich experiences to mine for learning and growth.

To my knowledge, we are the first graduate or professional department to organize whole programs of professional preparation around this approach to professional education. This is not a viewpoint being implemented by one or two faculty through a special clinic, sub-program, or course sequence. Rather, all of the structures, processes, sequences, and roles in the department emanate from this view.

I know of no similar efforts in psychology, even on a more limited basis. One previous effort came close to what we are thinking and doing. It was led by Michael Meltsner and Philip Schrag in the Clinical Legal Education Project at Columbia Law School in the 1970s (Meltsner and Schrag, 1976, 1978). For the most part, their philosophy was identical with ours, although it was couched in somewhat different language. Their venture differed from ours in two ways. First, as most of their students were in their early twenties and just out of undergraduate school, little attention was paid to issues of adult development. Second, and more important, they were a relatively small elective project within the larger law school. To some extent, both they and the project were seen as somewhat odd, unusual, or radical by the dominent culture of the Columbia Law School. For a variety of reasons, neither Meltsner nor Schrag is at Columbia now. Meltsner is attempting to implement the project's ideas as dean of the Northeastern University Law School, and Schrag is at Georgetown University Law School. Although the Clinical Legal Education Project at Columbia has survived, its shape and philosophy have altered somewhat. Major philosophical change in established educational institutions is very slow.

I suspect that we at Antioch New England Graduate School have been able to flourish because the graduate school is small and because we have an efficient policy and decision-making structure. Moreover, we are a relatively young institution with few entrenched interests, very few full-time faculty, and an associate and adjunct faculty group in the department that shares the perspective outlined here, or that at least is willing to experiment with it. Also, we have received considerable support for our venture from the professional community in New England, from colleagues around the country, and from the Council for the Advancement of Experiential Learning (CAEL), which has designated our program as model. It will be interesting to see how we and our ideas fare and whether and how we and they change as our doctoral program matures.

References

Bucher, R., and Stelling, J. G. *Becoming Professional.* Beverly Hills, Calif.: Sage, 1977.

Clark, R. "The Socialization of Clinical Psychologists." *Professional Psychology* 1973, *4* (3), 329–340.

Goplerud, E. N. "Social Support and Stress During the First Year of Graduate School." *Professional Psychology,* 1980, *11* (2), 283–290.

Gould, R. "The Phases of Adult Life: A Study in Developmental Psychology." *American Journal of Psychiatry,* 1972, *129,* 521–531.

Gould, R. *Transformations: Growth and Change in Adult Life.* New York: Simon & Schuster, 1978.

Gustafson, J. "Injury to the Self-Concept in the Working Group in Perspective." *Journal of Personality and Social Systems,* 1977, *1,* 39–52.

Halleck, S. "Emotional Problems of the Graduate Student." In J. Katz and R. T. Hartnett (Eds.), *Scholars in the Making.* Cambridge, Mass.: Ballinger, 1976.

Levinson, D., Darrow, C. N., Klein, E. B., Levinson, M. H., and McKee, B. *The Seasons of a Man's Life.* New York: Knopf, 1978.

Meltsner, M., and Schrag, P. G. "Report from a CLEPR colony." *Columbia Law Review,* 1976, *76,* 581–632.

Meltsner, M., and Schrag, P. G., "Scenes from a Clinic." *University of Pennsylvania Law Review,* 1978, *127,* 1–55.

Rioch, M., Coulter, W., and Weinberger, D. *Dialogues for Therapists: Dynamics of Learning and Supervision.* San Francisco: Jossey-Bass, 1976.

Schaffer, J. and Galinsky, D. "The Theme Centered International Method." In J. Schaffer and D. Galinsky (Eds.), *Models of Group Therapy and Sensitivity Training.* Englewood Cliffs, N.J.: Prentice Hall, 1974.

Seashore, C. "In Grave Danger of Growing: Observations on the Process of Professional Development." Unpublished paper delivered at commencement exercises of the Washington School of Psychiatry Group Therapy Program, Washington, D.C., 1975.

Singer, D., and Schachtel, Z. "Role-Relations Seminar and Application Group: Conceptual and Technical Similarities and Differences." Presented at the 1981 Scientific Meetings of the A. K. Rice Institute, Washington, D.C.

Stewart, W. "The Formation of the Early Adult Life Structure in Women." Unpublished doctoral dissertation, Teachers College, Columbia University, 1976.

Stone, A. A. "Legal Education on the Couch." *Harvard Law Review,* 1971, *85,* 392–441.

Watson, A. S. "The Quest for Professional Competence: Psychological Aspects of Legal Education." *University of Cincinnati Law Review,* 1968, *37,* 93–166.

David L. Singer is chairperson and director of doctoral studies in the Department of Professional Psychology at the Antioch New England Graduate School in Keene, New Hampshire, as well as a practicing psychotherapist. He is president of the New Hampshire Psychological Association and a fellow of the A. K. Rice Institute and the American Orthopsychiatric Association.

*As portfolio assessment matures, practitioners
continue to look for techniques that enhance both
personal development and the process of seeking
academic credit through assessment. Kolb's
experiential learning theory and learning style
inventory may have applications in this search.*

Using David Kolb's Experiential Learning Theory in Portfolio Development Courses

Michael Mark
Betty Menson

The long experience of Ohio University with adult learners, which dates back to 1900, when circuit-riding faculty offered courses throughout southeastern Ohio, has made us sensitive to the fact that adults enter or re-enter colleges and universities with needs and characteristics that are very different from those of eighteen to twenty-two-year-olds. First, as Thomas, Majnarich, and Lobes point out in Chapter Five of this volume, most adults have been out of the academic world for a considerable period of time, and they tend to be both unsure of themselves and unclear about the expectations of the academic environment. Though adults are usually highly motivated to learn and to perform well, they need courses that can help them to understand themselves and their learning styles better. Second, many are in the midst of major transitions in their personal or professional lives, and they are being forced to look in new directions to solve some of their conflicts. They are asking fundamental questions

B. Menson (Ed.). *New Directions for Experiential Learning: Building on
Experiences in Adult Development*, no. 16. San Francisco: Jossey-Bass, June 1982.

about identity and self-esteem: Who am I? What do I want out of the future? Why do I feel I have failed or that I need to change?

For these reasons, helping these adults to make the difficult transition from the world of work and family to the world of the university, giving them useful information and support, and empowering them to cope with the academic bureaucracy have been the main objectives of our portfolio assessment program since its inception. Until recently, the process was geared primarily toward assisting adults in presenting their claims for college-level learning to university faculty. Although the portfolio development course included exercises in values clarification and decision making, the practical objective of developing competency and learning outcomes statements dominated design and conduct of the course. However, as our faculty became more familiar with the literature on adult development, they began to realize that it was equally important for adults to complete the portfolio development process with a better understanding of themselves and an improved self-concept, both of which could help them to achieve other short- and long-range life goals. The faculty decided to add a new dimension to the course by using David Kolb's experiential learning theory and his learning style inventory (Kolb, 1976) to stimulate self-discovery and interaction with others. Kolb's experiential learning theory integrates cognitive and socioemotional factors in a conceptual model of the learning cycle upon which his inventory is based.

As Figure 1 shows, Kolb's theory postulates a four-stage learning cycle. The individual is involved in an immediate, concrete experience, which serves as a basis for observations and reflections. These are then used to build an idea or to formulate a theory, which may then be tested or applied in a different situation or setting. At each stage of the learning cycle, different abilities are required of the learner: concrete experience (CE) abilities, reflective observation (RO) abilities, abstract conceptualization (AC) abilities, and active experimentation (AE) abilities. New situations often demand learners to use abilities that are in direct opposition to one another. Learners must then choose the abilities or skills that they bring to bear on the particular situation. Consequently, most of us develop learning styles that emphasize certain abilities over others. Present indications are that learners who are farther along in their developmental growth tend to bring the various abilities to bear in equal proportions, although this has yet to be proved (Kolb and Fry, 1975).

Kolb postulates that, for learners to be most effective, they need to develop the capacity to learn through all four modes—concrete experience, reflective observation, abstract conceptualization, and active experimentation. Kolb's learning style inventory (LSI) gives learners an easy-to-use, self-administered, self-scored instrument that measures a person's self-reported strengths or tendencies within the context of the four-

Figure 1. The Experiential Learning Model

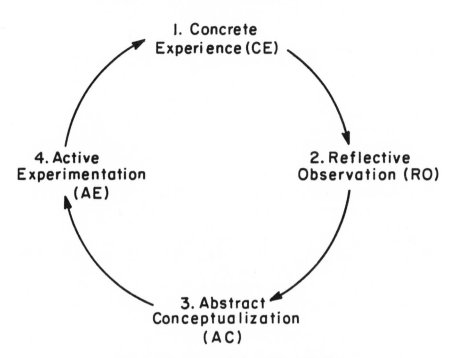

I. Concrete Experience (CE)

2. Reflective Observation (RO)

3. Abstract Conceptualization (AC)

4. Active Experimentation (AE)

(Reprinted with permission of David Kolb)

stage learning cycle in a nonjudgmental way. Responses to the inventory allow learners to be classified by their predominant or preferred learning style—accommodator, converger, diverger, or assimilator. Fry and Kolb (1979) have provided a detailed description of the theory and its applications.

In view of the research by Fry and Kolb (1979) on the fit between certain academic majors and the learning styles of students in those majors, our faculty felt that it might be possible to use the LSI to help adults to discover their own learning strengths and weaknesses in a non-threatening way, to compare their strengths and weaknesses to the demands of the fields in which they were working or into which they intended to move, and to stimulate their conscious efforts to develop new learning potential. In the case of the humanities and social sciences, Fry and Kolb (1979, pp. 85–86) found that "to contribute to those fields (history, psychology, English, political science), one needs to develop 'divergent' skills (concrete experience and reflective observation). This may mean developing the divergent ability of a learner with strengths in other areas (active experimentation or abstract conceptualization). . . . Would it not be simpler to preselect people who already possess the divergent capabilities these disciplines seem to promote? Perhaps, but in such a process—legalistic and moral issues aside—one would lose the creative tension between convergence and divergence or the chemistry that can be ignited when two such diverse learners are helped to work together. So, given that liberal arts educators are likely to continue to be faced with a mixture of incoming learner styles, yet turn out predominantly divergent learners, it is important to be able to understand their curriculum in these terms." Since the members of our adult population vary in age from twenty-five to sixty-eight and bring unique experiences from many different learning environments, we were convinced that the portfolio development class could be an ideal laboratory in which the "chemistry" among diverse learners could take place.

To date, more than one hundred adults have taken the Kolb LSI as part of the orientation process at the first class session. The inventory has been very successful in helping adults to begin the process of self-discovery and to analyze their learning styles as these apply to their educational goals. As we hoped, it has been a catalyst for group discussion on career choices and on the matches or mismatches between adults' learning styles and certain academic disciplines. Some of our students have reported back to us, with a great sense of excitement, that knowledge about their learning style has given them a better understanding of broader aspects of their lives and helped them to adapt to other environments.

For example, Betsy, an older woman in one of our classes, seemed very agitated and upset after we had explained the self-scoring of the LSI and its meaning for each individual. During a break in the class, she came up to ask for further consultation about her personal inventory. The next week, she returned to report that she was beginning to understand that some of her job problems, which had been very upsetting to her, were the result of a difference in style between her and her new supervisor. On the LSI, she fit into the reflective observation quadrant, but her current supervisor, she thought, fit into the active experimentation quadrant. He was impatient when she was slow to give a quick solution, and this was making it difficult for her to perform. Taking the inventory and analyzing her preferred learning style gave her the courage to discuss the situation in an objective manner with her supervisor, as well as an opportunity to re-establish some of her former self-esteem. She decided to drop out of the portfolio development course until her employment situation had stabilized.

Carol, who came into the portfolio course convinced that her goal was to be a special education teacher, discovered through the LSI that, while her strengths were in educational activities—she had tutored and volunteered in other educational projects while her children were growing up—she needed to develop abilities in new areas. Six months later, she picked up her portfolio and headed for a job interview with a publishing firm. Currently, she is enjoying her work as a copy editor. She gives credit for her willingness to explore new fields to the insights gained in the portfolio development course—initiated by the LSI. Quite apart from the role of the portfolio process in preparing her to present her learning outcomes for college credit, she reports that it also helped her to develop self-confidence and self-esteem.

Using the Learning Style Inventory in Portfolio Development

The preceding general introduction to the learning style inventory and the reactions of adult learners to it leaves several questions unanswered. How do the theory and the LSI assist learners to articulate their learning and to separate learning from experience—one of the most difficult tasks in the portfolio assessment process? How do faculty actually use the model and the inventory in the course? What are the benefits to learners in both the cognitive and socioemotional domains? What are the benefits to faculty?

Returning adult learners in programs that assess prior learning have usually had extensive experiences in business, community affairs, childrearing, and family life, but they rarely understand fully the developmental tasks that they have mastered, the ways in which they have learned, or the relationship between learning from life experience and learning in the academy. They face a number of questions: How do I fit the learning outcomes of my experiences with the criteria and standards of college-level learning? How do I review past experiences and extract the appropriate lessons learned? How do I connect the lessons learned with theories and concepts developed through scholarship? How can I equip myself to learn from my experience and gain some of the skills necessary for insightful theory building? How are my values driving me or motivating my return to school? What type of learner am I? What should I choose as my major? What are the long-term implications of my decision?

Faculty, too, are faced with numerous questions in the assessment process: Who are these learners? How do I help them to find answers for the personal questions that they bring to class? How can I get them to move to the point where they can present their learning for assessment? How can I help them to make the most of their return to higher education as well as prepare them for future self-directed learning? How can I give them the reassurance that they need to handle the academic environment?

Since extracting learning from experience is at the heart of the portfolio development process, students need to understand the assessment process and the relationship of life learning to course competencies. Our faculty, therefore, use the Kolb experiential learning model to demonstrate to students that both experience and theory play important roles in the learning process, that a learner can enter the learning cycle at any point, and that life and work experiences then call upon or bring out the use of learning abilities in one of the four quadrants of the model. Next, faculty show that the four stages can also be useful in actually developing a portfolio—reflecting on the concrete experiences of life with other adults in the course to develop abstract concepts about their learning that can be applied to specific academic courses in the university. For example, the model was used with a group of nine Methodist ministers who had completed a ministerial course of study and who were returning to school at the suggestion of their bishop to broaden their general backgrounds. These ministers shared a common vocational and seminary history, but they discovered through the LSI that they had diverse learning styles.

After a lively group discussion of the LSI, the instructor wrote the four steps of the experiential learning cycle on the blackboard: the group decided to use parts of their seminary training as one example of concrete experience. As they reflected on their past experiences, they generated a long list of activities in which they had been involved, such as giving speeches, meeting people, and attending special workshops. The task became difficult, however, when they tried to list specific abstract concepts that they had learned from these activities. Answers ranged from "I learned to understand other people" and "I gained tolerance" to "I became a better volleyball player." They were interested in the fact that they were unable to articulate their learnings in an abstract way, yet they had no difficulty at stage four of the cycle when they discussed ways in which they had used or applied their learnings in the course of their pastoral activities.

The instructor then assumed the role of a faculty assessor. (When possible, college faculty in various disciplines participate in this exercise.) He erased most of the learning statements; they did not represent assessable college-level learning. The group was dismayed, but the instructor was then able to lead its members into a discussion, with a variety of illustrations, of what was and was not college-level learning.

The discussion then shifted to the works of Neugarten and Gould (see the chapter by Marineau and Chickering in this volume), and information and theories relating to the various developmental stages faced by adults were introduced. The group discussed the importance of developmental tasks and their impact on one's personal decision-making process, and they discussed their own lives as processes of continuous change.

The students then approached the learning cycle exercise for the second time with added knowledge about themselves and the learning process. Starting with step three of the model, abstract conceptualization, the learners were again asked to articulate some of the learning that they had acquired. Although the list grew slowly, it was soon apparent that the group had grasped the concept of college-level learning from experience. For example, in referring to delivery of a sermon, they described not the affective experience of giving a speech but the skills and knowledge that they needed in order to perform effectively in the pulpit.

For both the instructor and the students, this was a mutually satisfying experience, since it enabled the learners to attempt to equate their learnings with those from specific Ohio University courses. As they looked through the university course catalogue, they began to find courses in which their learning seemed to be applicable. Philosophy 362, a five hour course on the New Testament, was explored for its appropriateness. The instructor discussed the learning objectives for the course and explained how the group's learning might relate to this course. Gaps in the group's learning background were discussed, and members offered suggestions as to how these gaps could be filled in order to receive full credit for the course. The same process was followed with other courses and disciplines. Since the ministers had unique backgrounds and learning in many areas, they were encouraged to explore other appropriate university courses.

The process described here, which we used with several groups of adults, led us to believe that a pictorial adaptation of the Kolb model could be helpful in reflecting what was going on in the classroom. Using the Kolb model as a base, Figure 2 was drawn to depict our instructional model.

Our experience to date indicates that both the Kolb experiential learning model and the learning style inventory have helped learners to develop learning statements that increasing numbers of faculty assessors are recognizing as worthy of college credit. One of the ministers, for example, had such extensive learning in the area of the New Testament that he was able to develop outstanding learning statements and documentation for the faculty of the philosophy department. In fact, his background was so superior that the philosophy faculty called the director of adult learning services to compliment the man on his performance.

Benefits to Learners and Faculty

Although no systematic studies analyzing the use of Kolb's model and LSI at Ohio University have been conducted thus far, we are certain that it is a contributing factor to the increasing number of successful student portfolios. The students clearly experience cognitive growth in the process, and they often report a heightened sense of self-esteem and self-understanding. We suggest that our anecdotal data should be supplemented by formal research in this area.

Beyond the implications for research, however, the Kolb model and LSI respond directly to three needs faced by instructors who are teaching

Figure 2. Ohio University Model for Portfolio Development

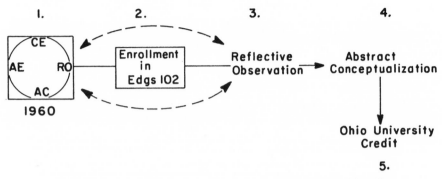

Adapted from The Experiential Learning Model by David Kolb

students how to construct portfolios of prior learning that will lead to the award of college credit. First, the model and the inventory can be viewed as instructional aids—techniques to teach students how to extract their learning from experiences, articulate those learnings, and equate them with specific college-level learning objectives found in course syllabi and course descriptions. The instructional model depicted in Figure 2 has been an effective tool in planning the portfolio development course curriculum. One entire Saturday is devoted to learning theory in general and the Kolb learning model and its implications in particular and to practice in writing acceptable learning statements, usually with the assistance of faculty from a variety of disciplines.

Second, the model and the LSI can help faculty to identify special characteristics of the adult learners in their classrooms. We are encouraged to see that faculty interest in the LSI and its implications for the broadening of teaching methods is growing and that faculty members are paying increasing attention to the combination of teaching techniques for their work with adults. It would be exciting to administer the LSI widely to traditional undergraduates and to conduct faculty development workshops on the need for developing diverse teaching strategies that respond to the entire range of student learning styles. Discussion of the Kolb model and the importance of concrete experience in the learning process has led faculty to take an interest in other adult development theorists and to receive training in life cycle research. "Transitions," a four-part television series developed by Ohio University and CAEL through a W. K. Kellogg Foundation grant to CAEL's Project LEARN, has been an important faculty development tool in this area, for it uses actual adults at Ohio University and Sinclair Community College to discuss their experiences in the portfolio assessment process.

Third, the Kolb model and the LSI can be of help even to students who do not successfuly develop a portfolio of prior learning. Many adults who do not pursue a university education will be able to use the knowledge that they have gained from the LSI in deciding what sorts of organized educational activities they will undertake in their future life. Even those who decided to pursue informal, self-directed learning projects will do so with increased understanding of their abilities and their attitudes about learning. Several adults have reported to us that the new insights gained through use of the LSI would not have been easily available to them without the course and that it motivated them to move in new directions both in their work and in their educational endeavors. Thus, regardless of the goals of the individual adult learner, the model and the LSI can provide important knowledge and foster self-confidence.

It is important to emphasize that Kolb's model highlights one of the most critical characteristics of adult learners; that is, the experience that they bring to higher education. Much of the literature on adult learning, in particular the writing of Knowles (1970, 1978), stresses that this feature—the widely varied, large accumulation of life experiences that adults have acquired—is especially important in distinguishing child and adult learners. Both the Kolb model and our portfolio development process reward the adult for extracting college-level learning from experience and provide a sense of structure for the process of self-discovery.

Before this instructional model was implemented, our portfolio development courses were taught in the following manner: Information was supplied to students, and students digested it. It was hoped that some flash of insight would make it possible for students to articulate their learning. Although portfolio development still requires some insight on the student's part, the Kolb model provides a systematic discovery method that seems to be helpful. A student can use the model to articulate problems. The student can say, "I'm having trouble moving from reflection and observation to the next step of the learning cycle." At this point, an instructor can intervene in a specific way with help to solve the problem. In our review of portfolios and learning statements produced by adult students since Kolb's model was introduced, we do see more analysis of learning and more sophisticated statements. As we have said, however, systematic data are needed to prove its positive effect.

Summary

This chapter has described one model and shown how it can be used to the benefit of students and faculty. However, the needs of adult learners cannot be met simply by improving one small part of the overall educational process—the articulation of learning in a portfolio development course. Larger obligations exist for institutions that are serious

74

about serving adults. For instance, there are points of intervention at which a university or college must provide adequate service: Information must be disseminated, and flexible counseling, financial aid, and library services must be in place to reduce other barriers. The value for adult learners of a program for the assessment of prior learning will be limited if there are no nontraditional delivery systems for instruction (evening and weekend colleges, telecourses, individualized degree programs, and so forth). Finally, we cannot serve adult learners if we do not know more about them. Very little empirical work has been done to identify the characteristics of adult learners who enroll in assessment programs. Perhaps we are guilty of too much active experimentation and too little reflective observation.

References

Fry, R., and Kolb, D. "Experiential Learning Theory and Learning Experiences in Liberal Arts Education," In S. E. Brooks and J. E. Althoff (Eds.), *New Directions for Experiential Learning: Enriching the Liberal Arts Through Experiential Learning*, no. 6. San Francisco: Jossey-Bass, 1979.

Knowles, M. *The Modern Practice of Adult Education: Andragogy Versus Pedagogy.* New York: Association Press, 1970.

Knowles, M. *The Adult Learner: A Neglected Species.* (2nd ed.) Houston: Gulf, 1978.

Kolb, D. A. *The Learning Style Inventory: Technical Manual.* Boston: McBer, 1976.

Kolb, D. A., and Fry, R. "Towards an Applied Theory of Experiential Learning." In C. L. Cooper (Ed.), *Theories of Group Processes.* New York: Wiley, 1975.

Michael Mark is assistant director of independent study at Ohio University and an instructor for the portfolio development course in its Experiential Learning Program. Co Author of the Independent Study Guide for Portfolio Development, *he is a doctoral candidate in adult education at the University of Georgia.*

Betty Menson is director of adult learning services at Ohio University. She is CAEL Regional Manager for the Eastern Central Region and a national leader in the development of experiential learning programs. As director of Project Learn for the Central States Region, she is presently coordinating the development of a telecourse on adult life career planning.

As adults rethink their career, educational, and life goals, new programs and services must be developed and expanded. Educational Information Centers could be the missing link.

Educational Information Centers: One Answer for Adults

Nina Thomas
Barbara Majnarich
Dianne Lobes

If the transition to a lifelong learning society is to take place, new programs and services that recognize and support the needs of adult learners must be developed and expanded. One critical and often overlooked service is educational brokering, which provides information and counseling support to adults who are rethinking their career and educational goals. In her work for the Educational Testing Service, Cross (1978) has documented the need for this new type of service, calling it the "missing link."

Until the 1970s, few such services existed. Within the last decade, however, the number of brokering services has increased rapidly; 465 are listed in the current resource directory of the National Center for Educational Brokering (NCEB). Located in urban areas, small towns, and rural areas, independently operated or sponsored by colleges and universities, community agencies, or consortia, serving women only or both sexes, all these services have developed in response to a community-based need, developing their own sources of funding and choosing their own range of

B. Menson (Ed.). *New Directions for Experiential Learning: Building on Experiences in Adult Development*, no. 16. San Francisco: Jossey-Bass, June 1982.

services. All also share a commitment to provide assistance to adults who wish to make educational and career choices.

The authors of this chapter were staff members of one of such program, the Educational Information Center (EIC) of Greater Cincinnati. They will draw on their experiences to give an overview of the educational brokering process and the adults whom it seeks to serve, to promote understanding of adult learners in different developmental stages, and to suggest some basic strategies for nurturing their growth.

The EIC of Greater Cincinnati was initiated by a consortium of colleges and universities with funding under Title I of the Higher Education Act of 1965. During its three-year history, which lasted from December 1, 1978 to September 30, 1981, when federal funding was eliminated, the EIC provided services to more than 3,000 clients. The vast majority of these clients were adults seeking to make changes in their lives—young adults who regretted earlier decisions to terminate their education, middle-aged adults who sought to upgrade their skills or to change careers, women who wished to enter or re-enter the labor market after years of childrearing, and adults of all ages who sought to enrich their lives through new learning.

While some clients needed only information or referral and would have eventually enrolled in an educational program without the help of the EIC, a large proportion of clients needed a broad range of services, including information, counseling, referral, personal support, esteem building, and training in such areas as decision making and consumerism. The second group lacked the confidence and skills necessary to approach an educational institution without some assistance and support. More than half of our clients had been unsuccessful or only moderately successful in previous educational programs, and they feared that they were too old to compete with younger students. Many were unaware of the kinds of programs available to adults in the 1980s, and they were intimidated by the very idea of going to a college campus. One middle-aged man, for example, reported having driven onto the branch campus of a major state university on four separate occasions before he ventured in to seek the information that he needed.

Educators seem to find it easy to recognize and understand such feelings and behavior in a seventeen-year-old who is away from home for the first time, but they find it hard to accept in a thirty-five-year-old married woman who is rearing several children, in a forty-five-year-old truck driver who has traveled the entire country, or in a sixty-two-year-old medical receptionist who has worked for forty years. Yet, these feelings are just as real for these adults as they are for high school students—and usually much more difficult to acknowledge, because adults are supposed to know and not to be afraid.

Before taking an in-depth look at some typical profiles of EIC clients, we will describe the data base from which these typical clients were drawn. Of the more than 3,000 clients served by our EIC, 63 percent were women, and 37 percent were men. Approximately one third (33 percent) were between ages of eighteen and twenty-four; another third (32 percent) were between the ages of twenty-five and thirty-four. Another 16 percent were between forty-five and forty-nine; 6 percent were under eighteen, and 8 percent were of unknown age. Clients included grade school dropouts (2 percent) and persons holding graduate degrees (3 percent). Thirty-two percent were high school graduates, 19 percent had some college education, 17 percent were high school dropouts, and 9 percent had a bachelor's degree. Significant numbers were high school students, college students, and vocational school graduates (3 percent each). The educational level of 8 percent was unknown.

Clients came to the EIC via two primary routes—either through mass publicity and advertising (44 percent) or through referrals and outreach programs (42 percent). By far the most successful advertising mechanism was the Yellow Pages in the telephone book, which brought 30 percent of the EIC's clients. Other media utilized were newspapers (7 percent), television (3 percent), radio (2 percent), brochures (1 percent), and church bulletins (1 percent). However, owing to the success of the Yellow Pages and advertising and to referrals from other agencies, mass media publicity was not used after the first ten or twelve months of the project. The part-time counseling staff was so overloaded that it would have been impossible to serve the additional clients who would have responded to this publicity.

Referrals came from a broad range of institutions, agencies and individuals. Referrals from the three colleges and universities that supported the EIC by providing 50 percent of its funding accounted for 17 percent of the EIC's clients, while other significant referral sources were the Federal Information Center (6 percent); personal referrals from clients, former clients, and staff (6 percent); and other educational institutions, social service agencies, lending institutions, and outreach programs conducted by EIC staff (3 percent). For 14 percent of the EIC clients, the referral source was unknown.

The greatest demands for educational information by clients were in the following areas: vocational education (24 percent), college and university degree programs (22 percent), financial aid (15 percent), GED and high school completion (14 percent), career planning (8 percent), college credit courses (8 percent), and leisure-time courses (7 percent). Other areas in which information was requested were job training and apprenticeship programs, basic skills refresher courses, and high school credit courses, registered nurse diploma schools, and adult re-entry programs. It was not uncommon for adults to request information and counseling in more than one area, so the percentages in this category and the categories that follow are not mutually exclusive.

There were a number of high demand referral categories. Forty-two percent of EIC clients were referred to college and university credit programs and courses, 27 percent were referred to vocational schools, 19 percent to adult high school and GED programs, and 11 percent to financial aid offices and sources. In addition, 9 percent were referred to career counseling, 8 percent to leisure-time courses, 7 percent to miscellaneous educational institutions (such as hospital-based nursing schools, libraries, and testing services), 5 percent to community-based agencies, and 4 percent to job training and apprenticeship programs.

Other services requested by clients included mailing written information (20 percent), providing telephone information but no referral (7 percent), and in-person counseling appointments (7 percent). During the last twelve months of the project, small-group workshops (4 percent) replaced person-to-person counseling appointments because of the influx of clients, while for the last eight months, the computerized Ohio Career Information System (3 percent) was utilized. Figures kept for the last twelve months suggest that the EIC also provided consultation services to an average of two agency professionals per week.

The descriptions of typical adult learners in various life stages that follow represent the patterns that we have seen the most often, but they certainly do not represent all of them. Although each adult is, of course, a unique category and will make the most rapid progress by being treated as such by counselors, some general observations may be useful to those who must devise appropriate strategies for assisting adults in similar life circumstances.

Young Adult Learners

These adults are often called *traditional* students, with the implication that the educational system was designed to respond to this group's needs. However, this is not always true, even for the young high school graduate who received little or no career counseling and who is now rushing blindly to college or vocational school. It is definitely not true for the young adult student dropout who wants to complete a diploma or receive a General Educational Development (GED) certificate as an equivalent. The potential GED student is hampered not only by a lack of information but also by feelings of shame and fear for asking too many questions, for looking too closely at the task that is being taken on. The past of such students is usually marked by both educational and personal failures, and very few people willing to invest energy in these students' future.

From their continuing failures in the employment world, some young adult GED students begin to acquire a consciousness that they must begin to lead adult lives of responsibility and productivity. They are beginning to realize, from practical experience, that a credential (the once-despised high school diploma) is necessary for their survival. Therefore, they ask for preliminary information on the GED, they ask which colleges accept the GED as meeting admissions requirements, and they ask what to expect in the employment market if the GED is used as a terminal diploma or certificate.

Charles, a very uncertain eighteen-year-old who used our services, is typical of this group. When he came to the center in September 1980 to ask for GED information, he appeared to be surly, cocky, arrogant—to have a "I'm doing you a favor by being here" attitude. Clearly, he was in the midst of an important life transition, and he needed a warm and accepting environment. By June 1981, he had successfully completed the GED and had enrolled at Cincinnati Technical College. His future options had indeed been expanded. What made the difference? Counseling and information delivered by a supportive person were critical to this student. The ease with which the obstacle posed by getting a GED was overcome had an impact on his decision to pursue further education. Solid information given in a professional and friendly manner helped to allay his guilt feelings and to build his confidence to ask for more information. This young adult, like so many others, needed someone to hear what he did not yet know how to say. With such students, an understanding of the psychology of young adult life transitions is crucial in the counseling process. This may be a last chance for the system to respond to critical needs. Much of the research (Department of Labor, 1978) in this area attests to the fact that clients who are rebuffed after an initial courageous contact become the unskilled, the nonvoters, and the unemployed.

Older Adult Learners Seeking a GED or High School Diploma

Although these clients often deal with many of the same issues that younger adults confront and although they can benefit from some of the counseling techniques just discussed, there are also some important differences, which have to do with life tasks and roles, that must be taken into account.

Older adult clients seeking a GED or high school diploma are often homemakers who have been forced to think about the future beyond their families. If they are newly divorced, separated, or widowed, the special counseling that special programs like the Displaced Homemakers Program can provide might be a good referral. Displaced Homemakers is designed to meet the needs of low-income women who suddenly find themselves in the position of needing to support themselves or their families and have no job skills, no resources, and no confidence. In Displaced Homemakers classes, these women learn that they have marketable skills, which they acquired in the home, and that they have the ability to pass the GED. Often, these programs are held at the same sites as GED classes and complement them, providing a supportive group atmosphere that builds self-esteem and provides information and career counseling.

Other adults in this category are workers looking for promotions or career changes who are blocked by the lack of a high school diploma. These clients are often male, laid off, and needing to put down time to good use. As increasing numbers of workers in the manufacturing industries are laid off, it will become increasingly critical for counselors to have a clear understanding of not only the developmental issues that these clients are facing but also of the larger societal changes that are causing displacement of semiskilled and unskilled labor. With this information, they can help clients to see that layoffs are common and inevitable in this economy and that the clients are not to blame for their situation. With a stronger self-image, clients can be encouraged to consider training for the new service occupations now emerging.

Adult Vocational Clients

Adult vocational clients need specific descriptions and economic information about fields that they hope to pursue. These clients' needs for training and education, we found, are often the product of financial necessity, a time of acute transition. Under its pressure, they often ask for information on the "quickest program you have." This is certainly a legitimate and typical request for one trying to solve a pressing problem. However, such clients can also be encouraged to consider other criteria in choosing a course of action, and they can be given a "quick" explanation of why this is important. Even if time is at a premium, counselors can help clients to explore personal values, consider the implications for future job and career choices, and even formulate embryonic career plans. Computer career information systems, the *Occupational Outlook Handbook*, and the *Dictionary of Occupational Titles* can be especially useful here.

These clients are often male blue-collar workers, while EIC counselors are usually women, as are many of their other clients. This can cause strain in the counseling process. That is, these male clients may not be willing to ask for help from female counselors, to respond to their attempts to prompt discussion, to accept their suggestions, or to think they know much about "male" careers. Some have even asked to talk to a man in the conviction that "he'll understand." Clearly, if EIC counselors are to be credible to a variety of client populations, they must have both an understanding of how adult development issues differ for men and women and solid information on occupations and educational programs.

Adult clients often test counselors' expertise by asking, either directly or indirectly, about schools in the area, requesting information on tuition costs, accreditation status, and the length of their programs—and about apprenticeships, job opportunities, and so forth. Clients whose questions seem interminable can be given the names and telephone numbers of contact people at institutions and guided to continue their search with them. If the information is reliable and the experience is positive, such clients may well return to discuss other questions and career plans, as well as refer friends and family for consultation.

Wayne, a twenty-six-year-old man with a GED, is typical of this group. He was interested in using his Trade Readjustment (TRA) benefits to receive vocational training. When he first came to the center, he was interested only in getting in and out of a program and seemed reluctant to discuss his situation. He entered Southern Ohio University, but he had to drop out for financial reasons. After his second return to the center, when he began to realize that more training at this time in his life might assure him of greater job security, he began to look at plumbing apprenticeship programs and to discuss a number of other options for future careers that could provide stability.

Most of these adults, both male and female, many of whom were blue-collar workers, felt silly or guilty about going back to school "at my age"—guilty because they had not sought further education earlier, insecure because of poor educational experiences in the past. Clients usually needed to discuss these concerns, as well as the societal stereotypes about aging and about acceptable and appropriate activities for adults at different developmental stages. They also needed to hear that large numbers of adults from all age groups are returning to colleges and universities and that many of their classmates would also be adults. Finally, they needed reassurance that there is no longer a proper age at which one goes to school, marries, or begins a new career.

We found that, in general, the older the adult, the more difficult it became to ask for help, accept risks, or discuss personal concerns and frustrations. Despite a certain level of confidence in their roles in the outside world, most felt that, in the educational environment, they had lost the ability to take charge and that asking questions exposed them to ridicule or rejection. Their self-esteem evaporated. Clients had often received so many rebuffs by the time they reached us that they simply expected another. As a result, they were grateful for our help and understanding. Because of the bad experiences that most had had with early education, these clients' concerns had never been heard. Our willingness to be supportive in reacting to their fears and insecurity was a crucial component of the counseling process for the members of this group.

Adult Women Exploring a Return to College

A significant proportion of the adult women who were exploring a return to college had been out of school for ten or fifteen years. Like the vocational and GED clients, they were very intimidated by their lack of knowledge about today's campus and by competition from younger students. In addition, these women were often receiving criticism from family and friends about their decision to return to college: "You know you're too old to go to college." "Don't you have a better way to spend your time?" "You'll break up your marriage if you go back to school. That always happens." "What about your children? Don't you care about being home for them?" "You're pretty selfish. Shouldn't you be saving the tuition money for your children?" This lack of support caused many of these women to be extremely defensive and isolated. We felt that they needed adult re-entry support groups to share their concerns and doubts.

Invariably, they also expressed a need for refresher courses that addressed study and basic skills. They found that these courses took place in a relaxed atmosphere that fostered self-confidence and the ability to cope with both personal or family concerns and the pressures of the educational environment. Informal support groups often developed from these refresher courses—lunch groups, study groups, and so forth. Returning women need to know that these confidence builders are available. Because their battle to return to school often took a great deal of energy, these women rarely had time to determine their direction. They were struggling to make the transition from the home to the world of work, and they were out of touch with the job market. They needed focused career counseling to learn about nontraditional jobs in such fields as business and engineering, which in their world were labeled "male" but which are now becoming increasingly open to women.

One important way of helping them to explore career decisions was to encourage them to think in terms of transferable skills from past jobs, volunteer work, church work, and workshops or seminars that they had attended and also to consider artistic and writing ability. Another was to point out that learning from life experiences could lead to college credit for portfolio assessment or challenge exams. Both ways allowed these women to view themselves and their experiences in a more positive light. To nourish their new sense of strength and independence, we encouraged them to seek out other women who could help them along the way—fellow students, professors, and university personnel but also professional, political, and community leaders. The university campus may not be the center of a returning student's life, and it is important for such students to begin to work with the real world of the community, if they have not already done so.

For example, Carol, a forty-three-year-old woman, first telephoned the center for information. Two months later, she asked for a personal counseling appointment. At this appointment, she talked about the numerous pressures in her life—a husband who traveled, four involved children, a mother who demanded time. She felt frustrated, pulled apart, uncertain. After completing an "Easing Adults Back" program where she found many others with similar feelings and problems, she enrolled at Raymond Walters College. She is currently a full-time student there, beginning to feel comfortable in the academic environment, and coming to have increasing faith in her ability to achieve her goals in spite of problems that she now knows are quite common.

Other Clients

Other clients did not fall neatly into any of the preceding categories. For example, we often counseled new high school graduates who had done well in school but who could not find jobs and who had no direction. In these cases, the calls sometimes came from worried mothers, not from the students. We also encountered thirtyish career women looking for graduate programs and financial aid. We noticed an increasing number of clients under eighteen, and of requests for career counseling and job skills classes. In our view, this trend is promising, for it may mean that people are starting at a younger age to ask serious questions about their lives and careers.

Clients about whom we have little demographic data were hesitant to establish a face-to-face relationship with a counselor, but they would use the telephone to explore educational dreams or plans. They seemed to feel safer when the interchange was impersonal and when they did not feel that they were taking up too much time. The telephone, we decided, gave them more control in that they could always hang up. Heffernan (1981, p. 93) says that because these clients have "poor information [and] inquiry skills," "lack . . . self-confidence," and "are unaware of their own needs," counselors need to encourage involvement, risk taking and assertion. The counselor's best tools with such a mixture of clients are, of course, the ability to remain flexible and open to the changing needs of all people and knowledge about educational programs and activities that can stimulate them to action.

Contributors to EIC's Success

Both from the research and from the experience of working with the National Center for Educational Brokering, we conclude that a sound understanding of adults—their orientations toward work, families, and education; the ways in which they learn; the challenges that they face in everyday survival—and knowledge of the life cycle and adult development theory are essential in providing effective counseling services. Familiarity with theory is not enough, however. Counselors in the Cincinnati project, which was located in an area rich with resources, found that many adults who came to the center did not know what was available. Often, they did not even know how to ask questions that would secure the information. If the center was to respond to the needs of an increasingly diverse population of adult learners that included women, minorities, blue-collar workers, labor union members, and retirees, its staff had to have up-to-date knowledge on a vast array of community resources and skill in helping adults to get access to them.

In our center, each counselor had certain resource, publicity, and outreach responsibilities, which were allotted according to counselors' interests, current knowledge, and personal contacts. Site visits were made to all the colleges and universities in the area, to many of the vocational schools, and to other agencies that served the adult learning community. Parallel with the site visits, counseling staff developed written resources in various educational categories. Center files on individual schools, programs, services, and individuals were maintained to provide correct and current information. In addition, each counselor maintained a personal file. The organization and updating of these personal files served as an excellent way of learning about resources. The Ohio Career Information System computer terminal was installed to serve clients who needed detailed information on careers and on the education and training available in the state.

Our referral service for adult clients was greatly enhanced by the establishment of an interagency cooperative in 1980. Its members consisted of representatives from schools, agencies, and community services that performed EIC service for center clients. Through a monthly newsletter and bimonthly meetings at member sites, EIC counselors had opportunities to interact with many of the people to whom they made referrals. Initially, relations with referral institutions were built through telephone calls, both into the center for consultation and out of the center for information gathering by counselors. We found that not only were we linking adult learners with educational opportunities but that the educational sites were also being linked as a result of our clearinghouse approach.

Another factor that contributed to the center's effectiveness was that staff training followed a clear self-assessment and mentoring model. It was not based on a rigid model that developed specific competencies that all counselors should possess. Fortunately, all the EIC counselors had demonstrated counseling skills in formal education, previous job experience, or community service work. To enhance these skills, trainees were often paired with experienced EIC counselors to research the intake cards of current clients and discuss with their mentors their ideas about resources and counseling strategies that seemed most appropriate for these clients. In addition, new counselors were always encouraged to bring client-related questions to staff meetings.

Based on our experience with the Cincinnati center, we suggest that seven factors contribute to the success of an EIC in touching the lives of adult learners: counselors who have self-direction, varied life experience, problem-solving talent, solid grounding in adult development theory, and belief in the value of lifelong learning as a catalyst for intellectual growth and personal development; opportunities for ongoing staff training and teamwork; an environment of caring and emotional support; an effective outreach and information-gathering system; solid relationships with the educational institutions and service agencies to which the center refers adults; strategies for finding support and delivering cost-effective services; and flexibility in responding to client needs.

References

Cross, K. P. *The Missing Link: Connecting Adult Learners to Learning Resources.* Princeton, N.J.: College Board, 1978.
Department of Labor. Washington, D.C.: Bureau of Labor Statistics, 1978.
Heffernan, J. *Educational and Career Services for Adults.* Lexington, Mass.: Heath, 1981.

Nina Thomas is currently a counselor with Educational Talent Search at Northern Kentucky University, and was director of the Educational Information Centers of Greater Cincinnati for three years.

Barbara Majnarich is freshman counselor at the College of Mount Saint Joseph. She has worked with adults in continuing education at the University of Cincinnati and as a counselor at the Educational Information Center in Cincinnati for two years.

Dianne Lobes is currently a teaching assistant and doctoral student in counseling psychology at the University of Cincinnati. A returning graduate student in 1980–81, she held an assistantship at the Educational Information Center, where she served as an educational counselor.

*Moving from an individualized to a group approach
and introducing holistic education strategies and
exercises into portfolio development classes have had
dramatic effects on both students and faculty and
lowered student attrition in the assessment process.*

Improving the Credit
for Lifelong Learning
Process with Holistic
Education Techniques

Brenda Krueger

Benjamin Franklin once quipped, "One of the greatest tragedies of life is
the murder of a beautiful theory by a gang of brutal facts." Adult development has been emphasized for years at Sinclair Community College, a
traditional two-year school with 17,000 students. In this case, the beautiful theory involved creating a program called Credit for Lifelong Learning (CLL) that would acknowledge and credit adults' learning from
experience. The program offered adults the opportunity to have faculty
work with them on a one-to-one basis in developing a portfolio of their
prior experiential learning. When the portfolio was completed, it could
be evaluated for college credit.

A primary attraction for adults to the portfolio development course
was the prospect of receiving credit for learning from prior experience.
The educators who designed the course pictured it as a laboratory where
the mechanical aspects of putting a portfolio together (such as principles
of valid and reliable assessment, documentation alternatives, and so forth)
would be taught. Yet, although as many as 1,000 adults entered the pro-

B. Menson (Ed.). *New Directions for Experiential Learning: Building on
Experiences in Adult Development,* no. 16. San Francisco: Jossey-Bass, June 1982.

gram per year and although students began to report powerful affective changes—self-image, effectiveness as learners, and life and career plans, among others—emerging from this seemingly mechanical process, only 50 percent completed a portfolio satisfactorily during the first four years of the program's existence.

These brutal facts led CLL staff to re-examine the needs of CLL adult learners. This re-examination resulted in three discoveries. First, a seemingly disproportionate number of students in the program were experiencing a period of major life transition. Second, most of these adults were not aware of all the dimensions of their transitions. Third, although the portfolio development course had been designed primarily to help students to prepare portfolios for assessment, the course was actually giving adults a legitimate opportunity to explore their feelings and problems. Eventually, staff redesigned the entire program in order both to heighten its affective outcomes and to lower attrition.

The new design worked. In the 1980–81 academic year, 79 percent of the students who enrolled in the CLL program completed a portfolio. Of course, since no controls were used, it is impossible to say with complete confidence that there was a direct cause-and-effect relationship between the changes in the CLL program and the increased portfolio completion rate among students. Still, three changes seemed to have lowered attrition: replacing the program's individualized format with a group approach, incorporating a series of holistic education strategies into the portfolio development process to make it more experiential and more affective, and increasing faculty effectiveness.

Analysis of the CLL Student

A re-examination of CLL students showed that the adults who came to the CLL program were experiential learners, but they were not all self-directed learners. In fact, many of the learning experiences that students brought to the program involved direction by someone else, perhaps a supervisor or workshop leader.

A review of former students' portfolios illustrated this fact. When the majority of these students described their learning experiences, they used such phrases as these: "I was required to learn the physical features of the 425 computer."; "My supervisor sent me to a class. This class was three weeks long, with attendance required eight hours per day." Thus, many CLL students seemed to be accustomed to a certain amount of external direction and structure and in fact to need that direction and structure in order to feel secure—especially since the CLL program was frequently their first college experience.

Moreover, the completed portfolios indicated that these adults would fare best in a learning situation that was as experiential as possible.

Historically, these people had chosen to learn experientially—from careers, volunteer activities, and hobbies—and they had actually avoided college. One student wrote that experience, not higher education, appealed to her. She explained, "I wanted to travel, go places, see things." Another typical student explained that he "had little desire to attend college." Instead, his "desires were to have a career," and he decided to attend college only because he "realized the importance of higher education as it relates to industry and my profession." Repeatedly, many adults' portfolios reflected that they preferred to learn experientially.

Adults' oral and written reflections on what happened to them in the portfolio development process revealed some other facts, too. There were a number of unanticipated benefits from the process. For instance, students reported that their portfolios were helping them to get new jobs and promotions. One such student explained that she was one of five finalists for a promotion that she really wanted. However, she was the only one of those finalists who did not have a baccalaureate degree, and she felt that her chances of securing the new position were slim. Still, as a final resort, she gave her employer a copy of her recently completed portfolio and asked him to read it if he had time. In that document, in addition to her work experience, she had described and documented her experiences and learning as a leader in her church for more than twenty years. She had also recounted the learning that she had acquired while helping her husband to manage and operate a large farm with a complex record-keeping system. Several days later, her employer told her that, until he read her portfolio, he "never realized she had done so much." She got the new position.

Other students reported increased self-esteem. One person explained that, although he had a high-level executive position, he had always felt uncomfortable about not having a degree, especially since many of his subordinates had graduate degrees. He described business lunches in which he would become silent or try to change the topic when a companion mentioned college. He was desperately embarrassed to admit that he had worked his way up without a degree. However, after completing a portfolio, his attitude changed. When he saw the finished document, he realized that he had learned as much as friends who had gone to college; he had just learned it differently. He discovered, as another student put it, that he could "look at the portfolio and say, 'Hey, I really have done something!'"

This process of looking at the portfolio—and, through it, at their lives—was extremely valuable, according to many students. They found that writing about their experiences reminded them of phases, careers, and relationships that they had enjoyed and found rewarding and of phases, careers, and relationships that they had not. This reflection led some to realize that their lives were not going in directions that they preferred. However, frequently they were not sure about the new direction to take or the new goals to set. For example, one man wrote about the many happy years that he had spent as a successful salesman. In fact, he had been so successful that he had been promoted out of sales into management. Writing about his life, he realized that his new "better" job was not nearly as enjoyable as his old one had been. Yet, he was not quite sure about the direction that he wanted to take from there.

Finally, another group of students found still another benefit to developing a portfolio. These students, all of whom were sixty-five years old or older, discovered that the finished portfolios made excellent gifts for their families. One grandmother reported that her grandson appreciated receiving her life story—her portfolio—so much that he actually cried.

Thus, it became evident that earning college credits was only one outcome of the portfolio development process for many students. Although students may have entered the CLL program to earn college credits, other outcomes emerged, and for some, these new outcomes became more important than the original goal. Yet, although the CLL faculty were aware of these extra outcomes, they had not made a point of cultivating them. Furthermore, both the structure and the experiential elements that students seemed to need were missing from the program. Between 1976 and 1979, the program had emphasized flexibility; there were few firm deadlines. Although students registered for a course called "Portfolio Development" to facilitate the process, this course involved only two or three group sessions and relied heavily on extensive individual advising sessions. These sessions were aimed at helping students to clarify educational, career, and personal objectives; develop a short chronological record of experiences; write about experiences and learning; and document that learning. Later, the completed portfolio was evaluated by teaching faculty, and college credit for specific Sinclair Community College academic courses was awarded when sufficient learning was demonstrated to warrant it.

Discovering the Group Approach

The CLL staff agreed that the basic elements of the portfolio development course were sound. It was the way in which they were presented that needed modification. The actual format for the new approach was discovered serendipitously. In late 1979, a key member of the CLL staff became seriously ill, and the remaining staff had to serve her seventy-five students in addition to their own. This situation forced one staff member to eliminate individual sessions and to work with twenty students as a group in a classroom for the entire term. By the end of the term, every student in the group had completed a portfolio. Meanwhile, the other

CLL students in that term received the usual individual treatment and, as usual, only about half completed portfolios. These figures implied that something different (and positive) had happened in the group approach.

Considering these figures, CLL staff realized that several different things had happened. First, the group approach required more structure. The CLL faculty facilitator went into each class with a planned and organized presentation. She also required students to hand in each of the various pieces of their portfolio on specific dates throughout the term. Second, the elements of peer support and peer pressure emerged from the extensive group interaction. Students helped and supported each other, both in and out of class. For instance, one older woman alternately encouraged and harassed a younger man into completing his portfolio, something the man probably would never have done if left alone.

The group approach seemed to deserve a trial on a larger scale. It also seemed that this approach should involve both more structure and more experiential elements. However, faculty attitudes differed. Some CLL faculty were uneasy about abandoning the one-to-one approach. So, intensive discussion, faculty training, and planning were initiated. Faculty discussion had always been an important element of the CLL program, and the faculty already shared their attitudes, discoveries, and new ideas at weekly meetings. These meetings became the forum where some faculty ventilated their fears and doubts about a group approach and others shared stories of their successful experiments with the new approach. Finally, the negative attitudes shifted, and the faculty agreed to try to work with groups of CLL students.

Prior to these discussions about the group approach, several CLL staff members had become interested in the potential of holistic education for adult learners. As stated in the first issue of the *National Holistic Education Network Newsletter,* holistic educators are committed to developing the whole person—"mind, body, spirit, and social responsibility" (Harris, 1979, p. 1). Holistic educators believe that the formal educational system should borrow from the field of humanistic psychology and from the human potential movement of the sixties and seventies to help people to learn "how to relate to their bodies in a comfortable and healthy way . . . how to think in an original, constructive, and creative fashion and to use inquiry skills . . . how to experience, accept, and express their emotions, to have self-esteem and empathy for others, to take responsibility for their lives, to clarify their values, to communicate clearly, honestly, and effectively . . . and how to be spiritually and socially healthy" (Harris, 1979, pp. 1–2). Holistic educators stress that the educational system needs not only to instruct students in job skills and academic content but also to develop their intuitive and imaginative faculties, the knowledge and skills related to social and political issues and processes, ecological awareness, and to think for themselves and act according to their highest values. "Students need to learn in a very practical sense how to be effective members of the democratic political process . . . not just in theory but experientially" (Harris, 1979, p. 2).

In contrast to traditional college curricula, which focus on cognitive development, the educational strategies suggested by holistic educators involve group exercises that promote what they call "interpersonal and intrapersonal development." CLL staff suggested that the move to a group approach in our portfolio development course should be supplemented by the use of several holistic strategies, which would be creatively incorporated into each section of portfolio development: the chronology and life history, the goals paper, and the learning description and documentation sections. These strategies, which will be discussed in detail later in this chapter, included guided fantasy, dyadic encounter, role playing, visualization, and affirmation exercises designed to heighten inner awareness and intuitive and imaginative capacities and to stimulate participants to a renewed search for meaning and purpose in life. The three-credit portfolio course, which meets for thirty-three hours in a quarter term, was enhanced by the group dynamics that flowed from the exercises.

To prepare for the new approach, CLL faculty participated in numerous workshops to develop their own group facilitation skills and to understand the concepts of holistic philosophy. The entire CLL staff attended a workshop facilitated by Jack Canfield, former director of the Institute for Holistic Education in Amherst, Massachusetts, and another conducted by Anastas Harris, educational director for the Del Mar, California–based Mandala Society. Both workshop facilitators presented exercises and strategies that they felt could be used with CLL students and helped the faculty to experience those exercises themselves.

Some faculty members were so excited about this innovative approach that they chose to undertake in-depth training to acquire other applicable skills and techniques. For example, several faculty attended a week-long conference sponsored by the Mandala Society. The CLL program manager enrolled in a year-long training program directed by Paula Klimek at the Center for Holistic Education in Newton, Massachusetts. This center not only teaches educators how to facilitate holistic adult development, but it also teaches techniques that involve students in the learning process—techniques that make the learning process more experiential. Many books supplied useful, adaptable information. CLL staff used Stevens (1971), Samuels and Samuels (1975), Canfield and Wells (1975), and Simon, Howe, and Kirschenbaum (1978).

Finally, when CLL staff felt that their own attitudes, knowledge, and skills were ready, they began planning a new structure for the portfolio development course during the 1980–81 academic year. They prepared a detailed course syllabus that included weekly objectives, activities, and assignments, and they developed a new, more explicit and detailed student guide. They also gathered and designed appropriate in-class activities.

Making the Process Experiential

CLL staff felt these in-class activities should be experiential and that they should help students to cope with pitfalls that could lead to attrition—pitfalls that CLL staff had begun to identify.

Very few students, the staff learned, had dropped out of the process because they lacked sufficient college-level learning. Instead, other factors had caused their problems. Three factors were particularly important. One was the students' lack of self-esteem and confidence in their own experiential learning. The second common student problem, as already mentioned, was difficulty in setting goals and thus in focusing and directing their energies and efforts so as to articulate their experiential learning. The third factor was students' lack of commitment to the process, which caused them to give up as soon as they encountered a problem.

In planning the in-class activities, CLL staff kept these factors in mind. Fortunately, they discovered that a single activity frequently served several purposes. For example, one of the first activities that the faculty used was a sentence completion exercise. In this exercise, students pair up and take turns completing phrases such as "The first impression I give to people is . . ." "A talent or skill I haven't used in years is . . ." "What makes me unique is . . ." "What I value most in life is . . ." and "If I really use the skills that I have the most of, the kind of work I would do is . . ." CLL staff learned that they could use this exercise to help individuals in the class to begin to form a support group. Another result was a budding sense of commitment to the process.

One student's reaction to the exercise was, "I told her things I've never told anyone, not even my wife." Another student wrote, "It felt good. I was more open about talking and wanted to relate to others how I felt. I usually don't feel this way." The exercise appeared to serve its intended purpose: It created a sense of camaraderie and commitment among the class members. It helped students in other ways as well. Some questions forced students to begin recognizing and verbalizing their abilities. This helped to increase their self-esteem and their confidence in their own experiential learning. Other questions started students thinking about their values and goals.

Subsequently, CLL staff used other exercises to help students focus their goals, exercises made experiential by principles and techniques borrowed from psychology. For years, psychologists have understood that the imagination creates inner experiences that can be just as real as experiences in the external world. One very simple exercise described by Samuels and Samuels (1975, p. 131) illustrates this. The authors instruct:

"Sit down. Close your eyes. Relax deeply. Hold your arms straight out in front of you. Imagine that your left hand is becoming heavy, very heavy. Imagine that it feels as if it were made of lead. Picture a heavy object, such as a book, resting on your left hand. Feel the weight of the object. Now imagine that your right hand feels very light. Imagine that there is a string around your right wrist that is attached to a helium balloon. Feel the buoyancy of the balloon. Now open your eyes." According to the authors, "Most people who do this exercise will find that their left hand has dropped considerably and that their right hand has drifted upward."

These results emphasize the power of the imagination. Moreover, the imaginary world has some advantages over the concrete one. As Rousseau said, "The world of reality has its limits; the world of imagination is boundless . . . not being able to enlarge the one, let us not contract the other" (1907, p. 246). The CLL staff helped students to do just as Rousseau advised—to use their imagination to simulate real-life experience in the goal-setting process. To do this, the staff used the guided imagery technique. In guided imagery, a guide—in this case, the CLL faculty member—asks participants to relax, using one of the many techniques that can help us to do this. For instance, the guide could ask students to take several deep breaths and to concentrate on the process of inhaling and exhaling. Or, the guide could ask students to imagine watching ocean waves move to the shore and feel the calming influence of such a setting. (Most participants find relaxing and the rest of the guided imagery process easier if they close their eyes.)

Once participants are relaxed, the guide uses a slow, clear, calm voice to lead them through a fantasy that can help them to utilize their own imagination and, perhaps, to discover new information about themselves. To help students in goal setting, the CLL staff used techniques taught by Klimek at the Center for Holistic Education and an imagery written especially for the center by Harris. First, since most adult students were unfamiliar with the guided imagery technique, the faculty person explained to the class that people frequently have trouble focusing on their goals because they cannot look beyond the barriers that they are facing, such as family responsibilities and money problems. Next, the teacher explained that guided imagery is a method for ignoring such barriers temporarily in order to find out what one really wants in life. Then, the faculty person led students through the following imagery:

> Imagine a day in which you are all alone. You have the day to yourself to relax and enjoy, and you are relishing the thought of it. You go out to collect your mail and find that only one thing is delivered. It is an elegantly wrapped parcel addressed to you. You open the parcel and find inside a beautiful leatherbound book. There is no card or return address identifying who sent the book

to you. Your name is inscribed in gold on the front cover of the book. You gaze at the cover and experience the feelings it evokes. Slowly, you open the book and flip through the pages. You realize that this book is the story of your life. You stop at one page and begin to read about a day in your life when you felt really happy to be you. You are in touch with your strengths and beauty, your inner greatness. Remember that wonderful day. When you are finished, you flip over the pages again until you come to a page describing a day in your life ten years from now. What you read delights you, for you find that you have fully capitalized on your potential and either overcome or avoided your weaknesses. You are a self-realized being, living as you would most wish to live.

How are you living? What do you do? What kind of person have you become? What does the book say about the way you look and feel, about your family life, about your environment, your work life, your personal life, about your social life, and about the level of your affluence? You now begin to feel that you have read enough for the moment and close the book to savor what you have learned thus far.

Experience how you feel about what you have learned about your future. When you are ready, open your eyes, and return to the reality of today and this room.

After the imagery ended, the faculty person asked the students to refrain from talking and immediately to write about their experiences so they would not lose the images and the learning. Next, the faculty person gave students the chance to talk about their images. The results were always fascinating. One fifty-five-year-old woman who had a bachelor of arts degree in political science had reported struggling for months to decide what career she should pursue, now that her children had left home. After the imagery, she told the class that she had discovered that she did not want a career at all. In her image of her future, she reported, she saw herself walking with her husband on an island in the Caribbean, helping to manage and spend his money. In contrast, one thirty-two-year-old woman, who had introduced herself to the class as a contented housewife and mother who was only taking courses for fun, began to rethink her goals after the imagery. She had vividly seen herself in the role of a travel agency executive. Other students visualized futures that meshed well with the plans that they had already made.

Finally, after the sharing, the students and the faculty person discussed how the images could be related to the students' plans for the future, how to set realistic goals, and how to work out plans for achieving those goals.

Overall, student feedback on the imagery experience was encouraging. One student wrote, "I thought this class was one of the most enlightening classes I have ever had. I guess I forgot how to look into the future. Today taught me more than I have learned in a long time." After acquiring insights about their own goals, students usually have the impetus to go through the rest of the CLL process. They know what sort of degree they want and what credits they need, and they believe in the value of their experiential learning. Also, largely as a result of the sharing in the class exercises, class members coalesce as a support group. They have friends who can help them through difficult phases of the process.

These friends help in very specific ways during the very last exercise in many portfolio development classes. In this exercise, the strength bombardment, each class member has a turn to be it. When a person is it, the person must sit silently while all the other class members of the class list the person's positive qualities. A rule of silence prevents the person who is it from responding with thanks or modest disclaimers. Strength bombardment is simply an opportunity to receive compliments. The result is one final boost to the student's self-esteem, which ideally has been growing throughout the course.

Both statistics and students' subjective feedback indicate that CLL's new approach to the portfolio development process has been successful. The CLL staff feel that the comments from one student make their efforts worthwhile: "I highly recommend this course to anyone starting or returning to college at age thirty-five or over—even if there wasn't one competency that earned credit."

The fact that the CLL faculty are in transition themselves has not seemed to detract from their effectiveness. In fact, student feedback indicates that faculty are more effective than ever. Students said that the course "opened a door that had been closed or shrouded in mystery too long"; that it "helps you to gain insight toward yourself and put things in perspective"; that it "has really been good for me and my family; I really have spent a great deal of time thinking about myself, which I have not done in years"; that it "helps me tremendously to achieve some of my goals by giving me insight on my own accomplishments and by building my self-confidence"; and even that it "is fantastic! I'll always be grateful I was directed to take this course." Perhaps it is actually because the faculty are open to growing and setting new goals for themselves that adult learners are so pleased.

One evaluator of the CLL program at Sinclair was complimentary about the powerful affective outcomes resulting from the portfolio development course but offered this criticism: The experience lasts only for a quarter or two, typically at the beginning of the adult student's study at the college, but adults ought to be guaranteed a continuing opportunity to reflect on the meaning and purpose of their lives. This evaluator recommended that the course be redesigned so that it could continue throughout the duration of the student's study and become interconnected in an organic way with the degree-planning process. In response to this criticism, the college developed a series of one-credit modules focused on adult life transitions. The Mandala Society collaborated with the college on development of this curriculum, which treats self-help health care, creative potential, stress management, interpersonal relationships, and life-career focusing. These modules are offered to core groups of students that reunite each term to engage in continued self-reflection and planning. At this time, fifty students are involved in these modules on a pilot basis, and a research project is under way to measure student attitude change. It is the belief of the staff that, when this is completed, the modules will be integrated into the traditional curriculum.

Students have not been the only ones to change as the result of implementation of the new approach. The faculty have also undergone some dramatic changes. It seems that in the process of helping students to solidify their goals, faculty members have discovered things about themselves and their own goals. Some have begun to use abandoned creative talents. For instance, one instructor reactivated his interest in playing jazz and helped to form a Dixieland band. Another began writing poetry again, an art that she had shelved years earlier. Still other faculty have decided to pursue new learning. One person began a self-directed Ph.D. program in holistic education, while another left the college to attend medical school—a longtime goal.

As Richard Bach (1979) wrote in *Illusions*: "Learning is finding out what you already know. Doing is demonstrating that you know it. Teaching is reminding others that they know just as well as you. You are all learners, doers, teachers."

References

Bach, R. *Illusions*. New York: Dell, 1979.
Canfield, J., and Wells, H. *One Hundred Ways to Enhance Self-Concept in the Classroom*. Englewood Cliffs, N.J.: Prentice-Hall, 1975.
Harris, A. *National Holistic Education Network Newsletter*, 1979 entire issue.
Rousseau, J. J. *The Confessions*. In T. Edwards (Ed.), *A Dictionary of Thoughts*. Detroit: Dickerson, 1907.
Samuels, M., and Samuels, N. *Seeing with the Mind's Eye*. New York: Random House, 1975.
Simon, S. B., Howe, L., and Kirschenbaum, H. *Values Clarification*. New York: Hart, 1978.
Stevens, J. O. *Awareness: Exporing, Experimenting, Experiencing*. Moab, Utah: Real People Press, 1971.

98

Brenda Krueger is program manager of the Credit for Lifelong Learning Program at Sinclair Community College in Dayton, Ohio. She has been involved with the program since its beginning in 1976. She has also been involved with CAEL and the Cooperative Education Association at state, regional, and national levels during that time.

*In a global age characterized by advanced technology
and a shift from a manufacturing to a service
economy, the developmental needs of working adults
are increasingly complex. The Gateway Program
helps adults to grapple with a bewildering array of
life and educational choices and to develop plans of
action for the future.*

Developing Self-Directed
Learners in the
Service Economy

Pamela Haines
Robert Schwoebel

Now that we have entered the era of the service economy, with its in-
satiable appetite for information, the golden age of lifelong learning
must surely be upon us. Certainly, the much-publicized expansion of
business and industry into the field of adult education is a definite indica-
tion. So, too, is the growth of small, private entrepreneurs who have
moved quickly to capture new markets. Surely, the proliferation of pro-
grammed materials, including growing numbers of computerized packages, suggests a bright new future. Even the efforts of higher education to
adapt to the requirements of lifelong learners, while not nearly so dramatic, hold out promise for new things to come.

However, some critical pieces seem to be missing. Why do many
people still find themselves unqualified for most of the jobs advertised
in the newspaper? Why do so many people find their current jobs un-
fulfilling? How is it that many adults feel ill equipped to perform effectively in their roles as mates, parents, citizens? Why do employers
report apathy, absenteeism, and turnover in epidemic proportions? Why
do they complain about a grim future and a static, aging work force, that

B. Menson (Ed.). *New Directions for Experiential Learning: Building on
Experiences in Adult Development*, no. 16. San Francisco: Jossey-Bass, June 1982.

leaves little room for fresh blood and new ideas? How do we explain that Americans are suddenly envying the "Japanese model," where workers are said to feel a sense of belonging and to place pride of workmanship over getting ahead and where benevolent managers take responsibility for the physical and spiritual well-being of employees?

We have made headway. We can point proudly to developments in the professional education and in the training and upgrading of technical experts and managers. But, what about the nonprofessionals, the people without a college degree, the great bulk of the service economy workers—that is to say, the vast majority of the population? In the industrial economy of the past, most workers required little education to do their job, and it was assumed that family, lower schools, and religious and cultural institutions provided the learning that enabled them to fulfill their other roles and life tasks. But, in a global age characterized by advanced technology, accelerated and continuing change, economic, political, and social instability, and cultural pluralism, the educational needs of all citizens have become much greater and more complex. The questions at this point crowd in at a bewildering rate. Indeed, their very number suggests that the fundamental issues and problems in our times go far beyond the need for a restructuring of formal education. However, even if we restrict ourselves to the latter, we can discern some prominent issues that, while needing extensive study, also call for immediate if tentative solutions.

Most of these issues result from changing technology and the concomitant reordering of the work place and our social institutions. People at all levels of the service economy need huge amounts of information, much of which is soon outdated. How can we educate people to keep up or retool on their own or with minimal help? How do we develop such an attitude toward learning? How do we provide the basic skills and keys to knowledge that facilitate such learning? In short, how do we develop self-directed learners in an advanced technological society, and how can higher education contribute to this task?

While most jobs now require some degree of education, once they are learned, they are little more than routine extensions of an automated system. Not only are such jobs boring to many and the skills thus acquired soon outmoded, but the training is such that it does not prepare people to move on to higher levels, and often it is not transferable to other activities. For others, the service economy has had the opposite effect, placing people in jobs that were formerly performed by professionals without according them the rewards and status that professionals command. The immediate effect upon employee motivation and morale can be surmised.

The inability or failure of large numbers of people to avail themselves of educational opportunities points to another set of critical needs that postsecondary education currently fails to fulfill. The need for better preparation in basics is widely recognized, but what few have realized or acknowledged is that many adults either fail or never begin because they lack the sense of purpose, meaning, and direction that makes the effort worthwhile. Is it not possible to provide an education that helps people to grapple with cultural pluralism, the bewildering array of choices offered by a society that has no cultural coherence? Is it not possible to design, deliver, and conduct educational programs that help people to develop their own theory for living and to plan and act accordingly? Can we not accomplish this in a way that enhances their self-esteem, self-confidence, and capacity to give and receive trust, support, and cooperation as they expand their intellectual capacities, imagination, and vision? Is there an approach that will help people to learn what they need to learn, how to go about it, and how to discern whether it is realistic and worthwhile to do so? Is there a way to do the job that speaks to people's personal and vocational needs, makes them more effective both in the work place and in the other areas of their lives, and helps them to demonstrate the proper relationship in their lives?

The Gateway Program

The Context. With such issues in mind, the Center for Contemporary Studies, a small developmental program at Temple University that had a decade of experience in undergraduate student development, set out to construct a model to develop self-directed learners in the service economy. We were determined to find some appropriate educational responses to the vast changes in our world; and to do our part to renew the social contract. Given cultural pluralism and a service economy constantly transformed by rampant technology, we wanted to equip people to put together their own design for living and to figure out what they needed to learn and how to learn it.

We did not have to look far to find an appropriate population. The opportunity was available at Temple University, in the form of its almost 3,000 nonprofessional employees, few of whom had found ways of connecting with or reaping the benefits of the educational enterprise in which they worked. Largely women and minorities, they represented the population that traditionally had been the least successfully served by higher education and that was currently the most sought after. As workers at a university who had access to six free credits each semester, they provided a logical starting place for the development of an educational model that could be utilized in other work settings.

While this group was not entirely a random population, its members included people engaged in a variety of services—clerical workers, ranging from file clerks to office managers; members of the housekeeping staff; skilled maintenance workers; technicians at the associated hospital. Sixty-nine percent were female, 80 percent were twenty-seven or older, and 58 percent were nonwhite. Two thirds of the entire nonprofessional staff had twelve years of education or less. Despite substantial tuition benefits, more than 38 percent of a sample surveyed in 1980 had never enrolled in Temple courses, and 69 percent were not enrolled at that time. A large part of our task, clearly, lay in making educational opportunitites at the university accessible to members of this group, not just in theory but in reality.

The Background. We began by looking at educational programs for workers at other institutions, including in-service training offered by employers and unions. We talked with union leaders, faculty and professional staff engaged in adult education, and experts in worker education. We talked with members of the university's clerical and housekeeping staff. Starting with the assumption that education can be a powerful tool for increasing mastery over workers' lives and environment, we wanted to find out how we could increase employees' use of the educational opportunities available to them at Temple University. (It was hardly a secret that the University had great resources no longer being utilized to their utmost by a traditional student population.) We wanted to find out what kinds of educational experiences they sought, whether what they wanted was already available or whether it needed to be constructed, and what blocks and barriers impeded employees from realizing their educational and vocational plans.

The outside investigation yielded a wealth of information on university-based labor education programs, union-sponsored job-upgrading programs, and general adult education programs of many kinds. We found no example, however, of a university that set out to make its educational resources accessible to its own nonprofessional staff, let alone any self-conscious effort to create a new model that fit the educational requirements of workers in the culture of the service economy at large.

The employees interviewed stressed the need for a strong support component in the program. They acknowledged concerns common to adult students: intimidation from the prospect of writing a formal research paper; embarrassment over uneven command of academic basics; math anxiety; doubts that professors would respect their maturity and experience; hesitancy to take classes with younger students; a heightened sense of peer pressure; fear of failure when studying where one also worked; fear of change and a possible need to repudiate present ways and values; the reactions—possibly the strong opposition—of relatives, friends, coworkers, and bosses; and frustration born of not finding ways of employing the new skills and talents once they have been acquired.

The need was clearly there, but what kind of program could best fill it? The best program, it was agreed, would provide more than career training or access to pre-existing college courses. Rather, it would help students to determine their direction, it would clarify students' life and vocational goals, and it would assist students in the pursuit of these goals. Our first policy decision addressed this complex of issues. The development group recommended that the Gateway Program should cover a broad range of interests; provide employee-students with the means of realistically assessing their talents, strengths, and interests with an eye to our changing world; offer them opportunity to do some practical life and career planning; deal explicitly with the barriers that had been articulated; and include a strong support component.

Although program developers assumed that employees would find a flexible curriculum of courses and workshops in the Gateway Program, they did not expect that everyone would want or need a degree, nor could the program hope to guarantee that everyone would end up with one. While some employee-students would opt for credit courses and an action plan leading toward a degree, others would choose to pursue personal interests and social concerns, sharpen learning skills, and enhance work skills. The tasks of the program would be to assess each individual's goals realistically and to make clear what it would take to achieve those goals.

In addition to meeting the educational needs of Temple employees, the program under development had several larger objectives. One was to integrate employees more fully into the university. Simply because they are the first representatives whom one encounters to the campus, they do much to create its environment and to project the tone and feel of the university to others. If a better understanding of the university's structure and purpose and expression by the university of its interest in the education and development of its employees can make employees feel a part of the university, we can begin to talk authentically about a university community. A real university community could prove far more effective than an expensive publicity campaign.

The second objective of program developers was to look at the Gateway Program as a model of contemporary educational experience that could be adapted to the needs of working people in business, government, and the social services. For all of its individuality and differences, Temple University is not unique; its problems are more typical than atypical, and the solutions that we reach should have meaning and use for other service institutions.

The Program. The working model that the task force designed consisted of six components: A personalized mentoring system that provided each student with a trained counselor, advisor, and friend who could listen with discernment and help students to sort out their choices, sharpen their perspectives, and chart a learning program that suited their own needs and priorities; an introductory seminar, in which participants could identify themselves as changing members of a changing world, explore their own interests, skills, values, strengths and needs, evaluate the educational resources around them, and develop strategies to implement educational, career, and life goals; a variety of optional course offerings and noncredit workshops in personal development, academic competencies, career upgrading, and development of the analytical and critical perspective required to cope with contemporary issues; a certificate that symbolized completion of an individually tailored twenty-credit course of study, which included the introductory seminar and other Gateway Program and Temple University courses selected by student and mentor as best contributing to realization of the student's goals; a series of faculty workshops for the Temple and community people who served as faculty, to assist them in establishing an atmosphere where information is not only imparted but where genuine learning takes place; and an advisory committee, consisting both of university educators and of leaders from the participating groups that oversaw the program and offered direction to staff.

The various elements of this program were designed to overcome as many of the barriers to participation in higher education as possible. The choice of university workers as the target population eliminated the most obvious obstacle, namely cost. Offering courses immediately after work and at the workplace helped to deal with time, travel, childcare, and energy constraints.

The mentoring system was intended to serve as the support component that adult learners so clearly needed. Designing the introductory seminar and other courses specifically for employees helped them to deal with the fear and embarrassment created by entering the college classroom at a later age than most do and with an uneven command of academic basics. In addition, both the introductory seminar and the mentoring system could speak to the central question of how to set direction and goals in a confusing and rapidly changing world. The twenty-credit certificate had a single purpose to provide employees with an achievable short-term goal. To those for whom a regular degree seemed so far beyond reach that it was not worth starting, the certificate would offer realistic motivation. Besides demonstrating that students possessed a body of learning, successful completion would bring a sense of accomplishment and solid evidence that it is possible to set realistic goals and to attain them. The faculty workshops were designed to sensitize faculty to the effect of global change on service economy workers and to issues of adult development in general, so that students could be assured that teachers would respect their strengths and be aware of their needs. Finally, the advisory committee was a feedback mechanism that could ensure that all the other components were working well and illuminate additional obstacles, ideas, and needs.

Our Experience. The Gateway Program began in the summer of 1979, with two sections of the introductory Gateway Seminar and thirty-two registrants. Now in its third year, all six elements of the program are solidly based, although additional amounts of developmental work could profitably be done on each. Four hundred employees have participated in Gateway courses and workshops, and 425 others have asked to be included on the mailing list. Ninety have completed the Gateway Seminar; the most active and committed core of participants comes from this group. Gateway is becoming a household word among campus employees. As well as attending classes and workshops, they bring friends, write for the newsletter, serve on the advisory committee, train to be mentors, and look upon the office as an all-purpose resource—thereby making Gateway their own.

The programmatic assumption that underlies Gateway—that if workers were offered a program that truly met their needs, they would devote energy to it, despite their busy schedules—has proved well founded. Increasing numbers of employees are realizing that this could be the opportunity that they were waiting for, the point at which they can begin to make a difference in their lives. As a result of their experience in Gateway, many employees have gained a tremendous amount of confidence in their ability to assess the situations with which they are faced and to set and work toward goals for themselves within that context. Their choices are varied: They have matriculated in different schools within the university, upgraded their career skills, gotten new jobs, married, straightened out intolerable working conditions. After years of confusion, hopelessness, or inertia, they have acted decisively on their world.

The Gateway Seminar. The introductory seminar, called the Gateway Seminar, is a microcosm of the whole program and its philosophy. The seminar breaks into three major parts. During the first few weeks, seminar students consider changes in society and the effects of these changes on the job market, the family, and other "life-size" areas. Students do fundamental background reading, and they are encouraged to relate their own experiences to what they read. The seminar leader is strategic in helping students to connect their own lives to the issues being discussed—to think about change and about how they can make changes of their own. Attention to values, identity, and life stages helps students to locate themselves amidst internal as well as external changes.

The central part of the course deals with the principles of life and career planning. Students clarify their values, assess their own interests, skills, and limitations, and construct profiles of vocations and life-styles for themselves. Everything is done with an eye to the contemporary environment and its effects on people and society.

In the concluding step in the seminar, each student prepares a provisional action plan, whether for a job, a formal course of study, or development of an outside interest. This section includes some consideration of the university—what it can and cannot do to help students reach their individual goals. Students also look at the process of goals setting and implementation and of building resource and support networks.

Gateway participants are not promised paradise. But, a well-led seminar will offer them help in sharpening the questions and honing the answers. Throughout, the emphasis is placed on developing a questioning, problem-solving attitude and on gaining the confidence and skills that will serve them long after the seminar ends.

The Gateway Seminar has been the most constant element of the program. Although the curriculum evolves with each semester of feedback and evaluation, the initial concept was sufficiently sound and well thought out that little essential revision has been required, and it has reliably served the function for which it was intended. Employees have consistently used the seminar as a starting place—a place to start building confidence in themselves, to explore new options and set new goals, to lay plans for implementing old ones. They have enjoyed the support of their fellow students and their instructor, gotten a clearer sense of their potential and direction, and moved on.

Their comments demonstrate this. One student said: "Gateway has been very helpful; it gave me the extra shove I needed to make up my mind about starting college and my career goals. It would have been a lot easier if this was available earlier. Who knows—by now, I might have had a degree!" Said another: "It has given me the will to complete a task I started a while back. Thanks for helping me find the insight and the added confidence I needed." One student confided: "I thought I would come here and someone would hand me a map. But now I'm ready to draw that map myself." Still another concluded: "What the seminar did was brush off a lot of cobwebs. The skills were already there; they'd just gotten covered over. Before, I was shy—there were a lot of things I knew I could do and do really well, but I sat back. The Gateway Seminar gave us a chance to be proud."

Reflecting on the seminar experience, employees see decisive changes in themselves and their coworkers. One student revealed: "As a result of the seminar, I got out of continuing education and into a regular degree program, and I feel better there. It gave me the confidence that I hadn't had before. After being at everybody's beck and call for thirty-five years, it has been hard for my family to take this, but I get respect and admiration from them as well as complaints that they miss me." Another wrote: "Since the Gateway Seminar, I have structured long- and short-term goals and have been accomplishing them, both in my education and within my occupation. I see that the knowledge and skills I attained I can share with somebody else, helping my wife plan, overcome obstacles, and build confidence to get a job and looking at the children—trying to apply little things about goals and skills on their level." Another student reported: "A girl in my Gateway Seminar just didn't know where she wanted to go. She was dissatisfied with the Pharmacy School, didn't have much social life. As a result of the Seminar, she really got her life together. She changed her hair-style, got married a year later, went on a lot of interviews looking for a job, and met a lot of people. It changed her attitude in her life—she went out into the world."

Mentoring System. The mentor is an old and hallowed figure in higher education, providing vital perspective, motivation, encouragement, experience, the human touch that makes the difference. Gateway mentors have all the qualities of traditional mentors, but they are also trained, and their role is explicit in the program. They understand that role in its historic context: They provide help to people in putting together their own design for living in an era that lacks an authoritative standard for making choices. As a first step, then, mentors hold conferences with their students during the semester and stay in touch afterward as much as possible. Some mentors assume this role purposefully and methodically; others are unable or unwilling to follow through so systematically. Staff also take up some of the load, making a point to be accessible to participants in the program, going out of their way to be helpful on the telephone, and making time to meet with those who need to sit down and talk.

In the first year, mentoring was limited relatively to ad hoc, scattered, and informal initiatives like those just described. The next step in formalization of the mentoring system came with a three-session training series in spring 1980 that was designed to give volunteers from the university community an opportunity to look at the basic issues in adult learning, brush up on their listening skills and gather information on the program and other relevant services of the university. Recruited largely through the efforts of one enterprising graduate of the Gateway Seminar, this group ended up consisting largely of middle-level administrators and program personnel whose jobs included some element of advising or counseling. Members of this small group engaged actively in the training process, were happy to volunteer their time, and subsequently were matched as ongoing mentors with employees in the program who requested help. In this process, the identity of the mentor shifted somewhat unconsciously from that of the traditional faculty member to that of the more modern professional helper. But, the process was not yet complete. The program still needed mentors, and the vision of drawing in the whole spectrum of university employees who wanted to help their coworkers had not yet been reached. The simple fact that training sessions were scheduled during the day, for example, made it impossible for most university workers to participate. The secretary of the Gateway Program provided the next breakthrough: "Why not offer mentor training as a credit course?" What could be more logical? A seminar held after work would be accessible to the nonprofessional worker; it would allow more time than the three-session series for the development of attitudes, background understandings, knowledge of resources, and confidence that are necessary for good mentoring; and it would offer credit in return for the hours spent obtaining this learning.

Program participants who had completed the Gateway Seminar were invited to learn to be mentors. Response was enthusiastic, and, despite the busy schedules of adult worker-students, the seminar has run successfully for the last three semesters. Participants have been fairly representative of the university's nonprofessional staff: Most are women, most are black, all are older than twenty-six, and almost all are without a college degree. In addition to secretaries and clerks—always a majority in the program—seminar groups have included a worker in housekeeping, a worker in the audiovisual department, a high-ranking member of the security force, and several starting level supervisors.

For many of these people, taking the Gateway Seminar was a key step in seeing themselves as capable of functioning well as mentors. As they describe the impact of the seminar and their decision to take mentor training, the theme of developing confidence and a larger perspective on their lives recurs. As one said, again and again: "After attending the Gateway Seminar, I feel more responsible for my ways and actions. I found out I was in no way the down-rated person I felt I was. I feel so much better about myself that now I am going into the mentor program and see if I can help someone else as I've been helped."

The curriculum of the mentor training seminar builds on the themes of mastering the processes of change, identifying skills and information in one's own experience, and developing self-confidence. It starts with the big picture of changes in society to give a context for understanding the dilemmas, frustrations, and needs that adult students—and potential adult students—are facing. It considers issues in education: the changing role of the university, the debate between career and liberal education, the growing body of knowledge on adult learners and adult development. Through all this, the underlying question is continually posed: How will a better understanding of these issues increase my effectiveness as a mentor to a coworker who is seeking to make changes in his or her life?

The question of what makes a good mentor is faced directly—and from people's own experience. Participants are asked to describe times when someone had been a good mentor for them and the qualities that the mentor displayed, times when they had been a good mentor to others and what had gone into that success. Role playing is used in mentoring situations to elucidate the characteristics of a good mentor, and a broad range of basic listening, counseling, problem-solving, and helping skills are developed in the process of feedback, discussion, and evaluation.

Everyone can find times when they have already functioned as mentors—both at Temple and in other parts of their lives. One student told us this: "There was a girl who started working in my department who wanted to take some courses but was having difficulty with her husband. She knew I was a graduate and started asking me questions. She started with the question: 'How long will 122 credits take to get?' I knew it shouldn't start there, so I encouraged her to take workshops as a start. She was giving me signals all along—I just responded. It's just a matter of listening to what they say." Another had this to say: "It wasn't anything formal, but when I used to teach piano, with many of my adult students, we did more talking than playing. This one girl used to come and tell me her problems. I loaned her books on nutrition and thought with her about going back to school. We talked that way every week for about a year. Once she said, 'Boy, if you'd been my mother, I would have been president of the United States.' "

Mentor training recognizes that some people, such as professional educators and professional helpers, are in a position that favors their becoming mentors. This position causes them to be viewed as mentors already, and they can slip quite effortlessly into the role. Other people have the same impulses and basic capacities, but they are not in roles that identify them as potential mentors. The mentor training seminar helps them to assume that identity openly and to place their impulses and capacities in fuller use.

If the participants in our mentor training seminars are at all representative, there is no need to worry about lack of breadth or vision in educational advising. Their perspective, if anything, is broader than that of many mentors in the liberal arts tradition—growing as it does from a synthesis of hard work to survive with intense appreciation of the opportunities of education: "Liberal arts teaches you to think. You get to know yourself better." "Your basic goal is employment, but you need more than narrow vocational skills to be the most well-rounded and qualified employee." "You need an overview, so you can fit things into a larger picture."

Seminar participants also take time to consider the staggering amount of relevant information about the university as an educational resource. Common questions that employees have about the University— services, procedures, geography, different academic programs—are answered, some in class visits by University resource people, others by participants themselves, who do research to obtain the answers. Thus, employees learn how to track down information and obtain referrals that they don't already have.

The seminar is relaxed. Participants are attentive and respectful. Both leaders and participants feel that they are exploring an important issue together. There is a sense of maturity about the learning process. People are both eager to get new information and aware that they bring a considerable body of experience to that process. Experience has shown that, with some training, supervision, and support, "natural" mentors can become superior mentors and catalysts who inspire learning among their fellows.

While it is clear that the mentor training seminar is working well, the mentoring system itself is still evolving. Our initial plan was to match trained mentors with employees seeking help. However, it did not take the importance of ongoing connections sufficiently into account. The externally planned matches tended to lapse quickly, despite excellent intentions on all sides. (Note that the only people who got attention were those who had announced their need to the Gateway staff). The relationships that prospered were built on existing connections, as when a woman who received mentor training became more confident and effective as a resource to other women in her office.

As a result, our emphasis has shifted. Rather than assigning a person with skills to a person who wants support, we are training as many people as we can, from all over the University, and encouraging trainees to use their new resources within their own existing circles. Many people who would never have articulated a need for a mentor are getting such help as a result. There is a trade-off, of course: This is a slow way to reach university employees. While we are pleased with our progress thus far, we are still looking for a more inclusive response to this central need for mentoring.

In our view, the potential for mentoring—both in the university and in the larger society—is unlimited. How many of Temple's almost 3,000 nonprofessional employees have been waiting for word from the outside that they can expect more from their lives? How many more are there in the larger community? How many would go far if they knew that somebody was standing confidently and expectantly in support? How many would grow to new stature in the process of helping others? As we scrap our assumptions about who can be mentored and who can be mentors, we are capturing the essence of the process of mentoring and unleashing a powerful human activity.

Other Courses and Workshops. The original vision was to offer a battery of courses that started from the point of people's own experience and perception of need, then built in the broader educational perspective. Building academic competence, upgrading career skills, and developing the analytic tools and critical perspective that enabled students to explore contemporary issues would follow.

The obstacles in this area have been impressive, and they continue to pose one of the major challenges in the development of Gateway. Many employees are reluctant to take a course unless it can provide an immediate, measurable benefit; it is hard to sell the benefits of well-developed critical and analytic abilities or better understanding of contemporary issues. With most employees very new to the college business, it is often difficult to get enough people to register for any course to justify running it. In addition, the center is forbidden by university policy to offer a course that duplicates the content of an existing course. When we look for suitable courses outside the center, we face difficulties posed by lack of control over instructors, teaching methods, and curriculum and by decreased contact with participating employees.

The present situation is a compromise between vision and obstacles that still have to be surmounted. We work closely with two departments—speech, which provides courses in basic communications, and business education, which provides typing, shorthand, business communication, and office practice. We offered successful math refresher courses, and we were experimenting with English until the university required us to refer employees to universitywide remedial academic programs. A newly developed course in citizen and consumer education has attracted considerable interest.

One early breakthrough came from a realization that employees are less reluctant to commit themselves to a lunch-hour workshop than they are to a regular college course. We first used workshops to test the audience for course offerings and soon discovered a great demand for workshops in their own right. We became increasingly aware that nobody on campus was thinking about employee development in any overall way. The unions kept an eye on wages and benefits, and personnel posted job listings, but employees were starving for ways to cope and ways to grow. Workshops in life-management skills—stress, assertiveness, single parenting, weight, diet—have been consistently well attended. Workshops on drawing and camera use are popular, there has been a small but steady demand for academic preparation, and people flocked to the workshop on home repair.

In some cases, employees are eager to move from workshops to credit courses, but they are blocked by university bureaucracy and politics. For example, our lunch-hour workshops could not meet the tremendous demand for computer education, but the Computer Education department is overextended and closed to part-time students. Despite hundreds of hours of exploration and negotiation by Gateway staff, a solution has yet to be found.

Now in its third year, the program is in ever increasing need of expanding its course offerings. More and more employees have exhausted our supply and are asking for more, but they are not quite ready to jump into university courses. Our current strategy is to conduct a university-wide treasure hunt to identify courses that would be available and relevant to the nonprofessional workers at Temple and instructors who would teach these students with respect and awareness. We have already found some—in social welfare, American studies, and sociology—and we are communicating with instructors about the program and preparing the way for Gateway students to those courses. This a timely move. It allows us to expand our network and to work with and influence an increasing number of sympathetic faculty, and employees increase their experience of university offerings while being protected from the worst excesses, abuses, and irrationalities of higher education.

Certificate. Any Temple employee is eligible to receive the Gateway Certificate on the completion of the Gateway Seminar and eighteen credits. Any combination of university courses, whether Gateway offerings or not, may be counted for credit toward the certificate, provided that the student and the mentor together have accepted the courses as contributing toward realizing the student's goals.

The certificate has served the function for which it was intended, providing a short-term, realizable goal that builds the confidence needed for attaining larger goals. At the end of our second year, three employees received the first certificates at a very successful and well-attended "graduation" luncheon. Many others are now working steadily toward certificates of their own with a sense of purpose and sureness that they did not have before.

Faculty Training. An instructional support system is a necessity for faculty who serve a nonprofessional working population. The faculty teaching seminar developed for Gateway is that peer support group. However minimal their formal preparation as teachers, college professors do bring years of teaching experience to the program, and this is an invaluable resource that can be drawn upon, shared, sorted through, critiqued, and expanded.

At the university level, there have been few supports, incentives, or rewards to encourage creative teaching. However, it is a mistake to imply that college professors know nothing about teaching and that there is a body of experts "out there" who have the answers. Indeed, there are specialists in various fields—adult learning theory, evaluation and testing, alternative teaching styles and methods, instructional technology—and practitioners need to tap their expertise. But, teaching is also an extremely complex form of human communication. While part of its complexity derives from the content of instruction, another part involves a whole range of capacities in interpersonal dynamics. Long before one gets to the point of asking how the computer or television can be used in a particular learning context, one needs to examine such issues as the impact of teacher attitude on learners, the influence of sociocultural factors on learning, and the implications of historical realities for the content and conduct of learning. Our program had two faculty training needs, preparing people to teach the Gateway Seminar and, in general, providing a forum in which issues of teaching this nonprofessional working adult population could be addressed and insights and experiences could be shared.

Initial recruitment proved the most important and difficult step. We were looking for people—from university faculty, staff, and the community at large—who were attuned to the strengths and needs of adult learners and to the larger context of change. Once we found such people, they were invariably delighted and refreshed to spend time with like-minded colleagues thinking, learning, and exchanging experiences on subjects of real educational significance. Where else can people from all over the university—history, elementary education, childcare, academic advising, statistics, classics, counseling, sociology, special education—gather together to grow as learners and educators? It is a powerful model.

The format that has emerged involves a three-session training sequence that prepares Gateway Seminar instructors and—with overlapping participation—an ongoing faculty teaching seminar for all who are involved in the program. While the ongoing seminar has suffered recently from crowded faculty schedules and staff attention to pressing demands, the need among faculty has been clearly demonstrated, and a model has been developed to meet that need.

Advisory Committee. The advisory committee component of the Gateway system has evolved along the same lines as the mentoring system. For almost a year, the only advice that staff received was purely ad hoc. Then, an abortive attempt was made to form a joint faculty-employee committee. The dynamics required for faculty and employees to work together had not been considered. As a result, the faculty—albeit with total goodwill—dominated the committee. Employee members—mostly secretaries—quietly disappeared. This beginning was sufficiently inauspicious that the committee was allowed to wither away, and nothing more was done until early 1981. We had gotten smarter by then. The new committee was formed wholly of employees who had been active in the program. They were relaxed about participating in this setting of peers, pleased to have their ideas solicited, and enthusiastic about helping to shape the program. In this form, the advisory committee has met on roughly a monthly basis ever since, and it has served a vital role in the program. While members of this new group lack the confidence and ease in conceptual thinking and the wide-ranging information that many faculty have, they more than compensate for this with their wholehearted commitment to the program and their firsthand knowledge of the hopes and needs of their coworkers.

114

How Do We Assess Our Success?

As we near the end of our third year, we have begun an intensive evaluation process, with an in-depth survey by an outside person at its core. Along the way, we have conducted formative evaluation through student evaluation of the seminar, periodic meetings with groups of students to discuss their responses to the program, a comprehensive needs assessment, ongoing discussion in the student advisory committee, regular critique sessions with Gateway Seminar leaders, and discussion in the ongoing faculty instructional seminar.

We are still learning about the barriers that higher education poses to service economy workers. People tell stories of going to register, taking one look at the crowds and confusion, and turning around and going home. Others miss the registration period altogether—it is simply not high enough in their consciousness. For several employees who had decided after their experience in the Gateway Seminar to matriculate, a minor bureaucratic mishap or unhelpful appointment was enough of a blow to their fragile new confidence that they gave up on the process altogether. Only chance discovery by staff members and thoughtful listening, encouragement, and counsel got them going again. People forget to come to class, or they get discouraged and stop coming, unaware of the procedures required to avoid a failing grade. Those of us reared in higher education are so steeped in academic culture that these attitudes and behaviors are hard to fathom. We have not fully realized the size of the gulf that we are expecting these people to bridge.

We also did not fully appreciate the diversity within the population of nonprofessionals at Temple. Just as many secretaries feel uncomfortable, inferior, and awkward in a class full of bright-looking young undergraduates, some members of the housekeeping staff feel equally out of place in a group of poised and vivacious secretaries. Although the supportive atmosphere of a Gateway class can draw in a confident housekeeper, we have not reached that population as effectively as we have reached others.

Because we are trying not only to provide service to people with an already articulated desire and readiness for higher education but also to nurture the belief that more is possible even for those who are not consciously hoping for more, the issues of motivation, mobilization, and support are crucial. Although all the elements of Gateway speak to these issues, there are still many people for whom it provides too little. Some promising initiatives in this regard include inviting people to go through registration as a group, with a knowledgeable guide; calling people up and inviting them to a class; filling the newsletter with people's own descriptions of steps that they have taken and changes that they have made; and encouraging people to find a buddy with whom to attend class.

However, the most promising means of reaching those whose dreams are still dormant or who have been so hurt that they have stopped trying is fellow employees who have discovered that they are bigger than they had thought. Jean convinces Katrina to try the Gateway Seminar. Lucy walks her two coworkers through registration and enrollment. Peggy calls all the women whom she thinks she can convince to take shorthand. It is a slow process, but it does work.

Conclusions and New Directions

We are convinced that this program has implications that go far beyond meeting the needs of one particular population at one university. We believe that it is a highly significant response to the still unstudied and largely unmet needs of nonprofessional workers in a postindustrial economy. With the support of the Fund for the Improvement of Post-secondary Education, the Gateway Seminar has just been adapted by CLEO (Compact for Lifelong Educational Opportunities), a consortium of colleges and universities in the Philadelphia area, for use with employees in a variety of job settings. Although the mentoring system and other pieces of the Gateway program will be more difficult to implement in nonuniversity employment settings, the Employee Action Plan Seminar developed by CLEO, like the core Gateway Seminar, assumes that the culture and problems of service economy workers, profoundly different as they are from the culture and problems of industrial workers, need to be understood if educational institutions are to play a role in helping workers to realize their potential and power. Thus, the Gateway concept is already serving as both as a practical model that educators can adapt and as a vehicle for the conduct of original research about one of the central issues in today's society.

*Pamela Haines is associate director of the Gateway
Program, an educational program for the clerical,
technical, and service staff of Temple University. She
has worked in the field of adult education for ten years
at Temple University, Community College of Philadelphia,
and with private groups.*

*Robert Schwoebel is professor of history and director of the
Center for Contemporary Studies, Temple University. In 1971
he received the Danforth Foundation's E. Harris Harbison
award for gifted teaching, and he is currently working with
CLEO Regional Consortium of Colleges and Universities in
the Delaware Valley.*

The editor summarizes the volume and provides
sources of further information.

Conclusion and
Additional Resources

Betty Menson

The authors of the chapters in this sourcebook have described a variety of
programs and strategies for effective response to the developmental needs
of adult learners—redesigning prior learning assessment programs; providing better counseling and information services; integrating theory,
practice, and personal exploration into the formal curriculum; establishing a mentoring system and a seminar for addressing human development
in a changing society; and creating a voluntary campus support network
for returning women students. Although the programs and the settings in
which they were established are very different—ranging from an urban
community college and a community-based brokering service to a rural
university—certain common themes emerge.

    First, faculty and staff development is essential for the successful
adaptation of adult learner programs. Faculty and staff need to understand the differences between adult learners and traditional undergraduates, and this understanding must go well beyond the conventional
wisdom that adults have families and jobs and need courses at flexible
times and places. Marienau and Chickering second Cross in saying that
only as adult educators begin to think about the special characteristics of
adult learners and the various contexts within which their learning takes
place will the profession of adult education advance.

B. Menson (Ed.). *New Directions for Experiential Learning: Building on*
Experiences in Adult Development, no. 16. San Francisco: Jossey-Bass, June 1982.

The majority of the adults who choose to return to a college or university are probably in the midst of a life transition. They are likely to bring the effects of this transition to the classroom or to the assessment process. These two concepts are central to faculty training in adult development. Faculty need to be aware of the difficulty that adults may have when they discover that they are closer in age, interests, and life issues—but not in status—to the faculty than to their fellow students. Faculty also need to recognize that adult learners are fulfilling a variety of roles, just as they are themselves, and that the student role is necessarily and appropriately a part-time role, whether the adult is enrolled for full-time or part-time course work. For these reasons, faculty training sessions should center on something concrete, such as improving the quality of the assessment process for prior learning, but they must also allow for discussion of the developmental needs of adults. One good technique brings articulate adult learners to faculty training sessions to answer questions and tell their stories.

Second, assessment of prior learning and other related adult learning programs should not be viewed or conducted as a credentialing process; instead, it should consciously foster human development and self-directed learning. As several of the authors report, the personal growth experienced by adults who participate in portfolio development courses, Gateway Seminars, or the like is as valuable to them as the degree itself, if not more so. This theme is consistent with Knapp's (1981) reports of adult learners and with the recommendations of Knapp and Gardiner (1981) recommendations for the reform of assessment programs: "The assessment process should be designed so that credit granting is only one of the objectives of the assessment process, with building faculty and learner skills in evaluating and planning learning as the major goal. In order to achieve this goal, educational planning courses should be part of the curriculum" (Knapp and Gardiner, 1981, p. 30).

Third, there is a growing need to conduct adult development research, to clarify and analyze the differences between the current schools of adult development theory, and to build effective models for relating theory to program implementation. As the chapters in this volume make clear, practitioners have made borrowings from the literature, but they have rarely attempted to incorporate the broad perspective called for by Haines and Schwoebel in Chapter Seven or by Singer in Chapter Three. Unfortunately, the practitioners who have the dedication and enthusiasm to work for institutional change are rarely the research-oriented individuals. Moreover, reliable data on adult learners are difficult to collect, because of the many demands on adults' time. Nevertheless, the body of research data is growing, and its potential for informing teaching and program design is enormous.

Fourth, institutions must stop treating adult education as a peripheral enterprise and integrate a concern for lifelong learning and human development into their philosophy, mission, and planning process—and ultimately their resource allocations. This will require adult learning practitioners to examine the feasibility of integrating their services and programs into the larger institution. Although involvement of faculty departments in the assessment of prior learning process makes the development process take longer, the resulting program is stronger in the long run and less vulnerable to budget cuts and political whim. Practitioners interested in fostering adult development must gain the commitment of the institution for educational and philosophical reasons as well as for economic ones, and this will require a radical shift in approach for many who are accustomed to managing their adult learning or continuing education programs small, not as academic divisions but as semiautonomous businesses.

As the first step in obtaining institutional commitment to serving adults, adult learning practitioners could introduce the questions in the chapter by Marienau and Chickering as discussion items for academic and budget planning, for the issue that these authors raise is fundamental: As practitioners, we cannot be content with "a few new approaches or altered practices. Tantalizing options for learning may be available in a few areas, while major restrictions persist in others. In too many cases, then, we have managed only to bring students a bit further along in the system before they encounter severe blocks to achieving their full potential" (Lindquist and Marienau, 1981).

I am convinced that adult learning programs and services, especially portfolio assessment, will survive and flourish in a majority of institutions during the 1980s. For the most part, however, these programs will reach the same population that higher education has reached in the past—the middle class. If we are to serve a more diverse student body, then our support services, marketing strategies, and program designs need to be re-examined and modified to meet new needs, and our current focus on enrollment in degree programs may need to diminish.

The conclusion of a report of the Phi Delta Kappa Commission on Lifelong Learning (Overly and others, 1980) can serve as a useful set of organizing principles for the future:

> We believe that every person has the capability, the right, and the responsibility to become a lifelong learner and that the environment should be supportive of people in this task. We believe that the opportunities to continue to learn throughout life should not be limited by location, economics, or other restrictions.
>
> We believe that society has the right and responsibility to designate certain competencies that allow persons to function in

that society. At the same time, we also believe that individuals must take increasing responsibility for their own goal-directed learning.

We believe that the current system of schools is an essential part of the support system for lifelong learning but that it does not have a monopoly on providing that learning. We believe that the promotion of lifelong learning will require new kinds of institutions and better use of existing institutions.

We also believe that most people need meaningful work— work that goes beyond simply a job and may include service to others, esthetic development, and development of a satisfying life-style. The thrust of lifelong learning should encourage this expanding view of work.

We believe that we are living in a time of rapid societal changes that demand that individuals learn to cope with an emerging society to which they will both contribute and react.

We believe that the changing nature of society requires that persons learn not only to cope with change but to have a role in shaping change [Overly and others, 1980, p. vii].

These goals imply that those of us in colleges and universities must take responsibility for reshaping our institutions in fundamental ways. It is not enough merely to put a new name on something that is already in place. It is time, as Marineau and Chickering say, to move from rhetoric to reality.

References

Knapp, J. *New Directions for Experiential Learning: Financing and Implementing Prior Learning Assessment,* no. 14. San Francisco: Jossey-Bass, 1981.

Lindquist, J., and Marienau, C. *Turning Colleges Toward Adults.* Memphis, Tenn.: Institute for Academic Improvement, Center for the Study of Higher Education, 1981.

Overly, N. V., McQuigg, R. B., Silvernail, D. L., and Coppedge, F. L. "A Model For Lifelong Learning: Phi Delta Kappa, Commission on Lifelong Learning 1980." *Phi Delta Kappan,* 1980.

Additional Resources

Independent of the references in the chapters of this sourcebook, I am including a list of basic resources in the areas of adult development, re-entry women, educational information centers, and lifelong learning. I have found these works to be extremely readable and useful.

Arbeiter, S., Aslanian, C. B., Schnierbeck, F. A., and Brickell, H. M. *Forty Million Americans in Career Transition.* Princeton, N.J.: College Board, 1978.

The report of a survey of the career transition needs of a representative sample of adults in transition conducted by the College Board in 1975 and 1976. An excellent resource for those planning or thinking about meeting adult needs.

Aslanian, C. B., and Brickell, H. B. *Americans in Transition: Life Changes as Reasons for Adult Learning.* Princeton, N.J.: College Board, 1980.

An excellent handbook examining the correlation between the current return-to-school movement of adults and its relationship to various social and economic developments. The book is based on interviews with more than 2,000 men and women that center on the question "Why do adults learn?"

Association of American Colleges. *Monograph on Re-entry Women from a Project on the Status and Education of Women.* Washington, D.C.: Association of American Colleges, 1980.

Prepared under a grant from the Women's Educational Equity Act Program, these monographs deal in great detail with issues discussed in Holt's chapter, such as barriers, student services, and financial aid.

Chickering, A., and Associates. *The Modern American College: Responding to the New Realities of Diverse Students and a Changing Society.* San Francisco: Jossey-Bass, 1981.

An excellent resource book on the concept of adult life cycle development and the ways in which colleges and universities can respond and encourage change, with contributions by a variety of experts. This book is invaluable for educators who are considering increasing their institution's emphasis on the adult market and who are looking for concise but varied expertise.

Cross, K. P. *Adults as Learners: Increasing Participation and Facilitating Learning.* San Francisco: Jossey-Bass, 1981.

A comprehensive book on the adult learner prepared after a review of books, articles, and reports from the field. Cross explains who adult learners are and how they want to learn. She develops two new models, one for understanding the motivation of adults and the other for organizing knowledge about their characteristics and circumstances.

Cross, K. P. *The Missing Link: Connecting Adult Learners to Learning Resources.* Princeton, N.J.: College Board, 1978.

Practical suggestions on assisting adults to tap resources that they need through use of information networks.

Goodman, E. *Turning Points*. New York: Doubleday, 1979.

A national columnist writes about the adult life cycle crises that come not from the aging process but from social forces. Goodman writes about people like most of us; her journalistic style and her use of real people make this work quite accessible.

Gould, R. L. *Transformations*. New York: Simon & Schuster, 1978.

A very readable book, written by a psychiatrist, that deals with the evolution of adult consciousness as we remove the constraints and ties of childhood messages. Based on Gould's own studies of almost 1,000 people of varying ages and backgrounds, it lays particular emphasis on coping with crisis and change.

Gross, R. E. *The Lifelong Learner*. New York: Simon & Schuster, 1977.

An excellent handbook for assisting the lifelong learner to use resources and the system to gain personal and career goals.

Harrington, F. H. *The Future of Adult Education: New Responsibilities of Colleges and Universities*. San Francisco: Jossey-Bass, 1977.

For some, a "Bible" of adult education, this work describes a full range of adult education programs, associated problems, and recommendations for management, funding, and so forth. Very valuable for beginners.

Knowles, M. E. *The Adult Learner: A Neglected Species*. Houston: Gulf, 1978.

A very readable and scholarly work. Knowles contrasts adult learning theories and practices to child learning theories and practices. Whether one is familiar with his theories or not, it is an excellent resource for developing meaningful adult programs and guidelines for selecting and training teachers.

Knox, A. *Adult Development and Learning: A Handbook on Individual Growth and Competence in the Adult Years for Education and the Helping Professions*. San Francisco: Jossey-Bass, 1977.

A synthesis of more than 1,000 studies of adult development and learning from a variety of fields.

Levinson, D. J., and others. *The Seasons of a Man's Life*. New York: Knopf, 1978.

One of the best-known books in the area of adult development, it is based on a ten-year study of a group of forty men done by Levinson and his associates over a period of several years. Their prime aim, say the authors, was to "create a developmental perspective on adulthood in men." Almost a classic in the field, this book is one of the most popular.

Lowenthal, M. F., Thurner, M., Chiriboga, D., and Associates. *Four Stages of Life: A Comparative Study of Women and Men Facing Transition.* San Francisco: Jossey-Bass, 1975.

A pioneering book on the sociopsychological dilemma and resources of women and men confronting the various transitions of adult life. The concepts and findings of the study challenge some prevailing theories of adult development. This work is particularly meaningful for those who are interested in the psychological and social factors that help men to adapt and not women or that influence women and not men.

McLeish, J.A.B. *The Ulyssean Adult: Creativity in the Middle and Later Years.* Scarborough, Ontario, Canada: McGraw-Hill Ryerson, 1976.

A particularly important resource for those who are dealing with adult learners in the late years. Drawing on his extensive knowledge of the literature and the creative arts and more than a quarter century of experience and work in the area of adult learning, McLeish leaves the reader with a sense that life is forever an adventure.

Moore, K. M., and Wollitzer, P. *Women in Higher Education: A Comtemporary Bibliography.* Washington, D.C.: Association of American Colleges, 1979.

An annotated bibliography of research on academic women published between 1970 and 1978 that includes fifteen entries under "Adult Women in Higher Education." A time-saver for those interested in research on academic women through 1978. Available from National Association for Women Deans, Administrators, and Counselors, 1625 I Street N.W., Suite 624A, Washington, D.C. 20006.

Peterson, R. E., and Associates. *Lifelong Learning in America: An Overview of Current Practices, Available Resources, and Future Prospects.* San Francisco: Jossey-Bass, 1979.

A valuable resource that brings together in one volume information from a variety of sources about the wide range of policies and practices for lifelong learning in America. Since it was published in 1979 and the field is growing rapidly, the book will soon need to be updated.

Scarf, M. *Unfinished Business: Pressure Points in the Lives of Women.* New York: Doubleday, 1980.

Particularly appropriate for a counseling staff or a women's network group, this book is engrossing to read and would be an invaluable aid to both men and women who are working with returning women.

Schrall, M. *Limits: A Search for New Values.* New York: Clarkson Potter, 1981.

Using firsthand accounts, statistics, and extensive research, Schrall describe the vacuum that people feel as they search for new values to replace older values on marriage, family, work, and children. Filled with ideas appropriate to these challenging times, this book is a must both for those who are floundering and those who are concerned for the direction that the world is taking.

Sheehy, G. *Passages: Predictable Crises of Adult Life.* New York: Dutton, 1976.

This easy-to-read, best-selling report of people in a variety of life stages tends to emphasize chronological ages and periods as times of predictable crisis.

Tyler, L. E. *Individuality: Human Possibilities and Personal Choice in the Psychological Development of Men and Women.* San Francisco: Jossey-Bass, 1978.

A new framework for understanding human individuality that has its basis in the choices that people make—what they will learn, where they will be, who they will associate with. Tyler's idea has enormous implications for adult program development. Since Tyler is a recognized authority in the counseling field, her approach has special implications for those in the adult student personnel field.

Yaneklovich, D. *New Rules: Searching for Self-Fulfillment in a World Turned Upside Down.* New York: Random House, 1981.

Combining life histories and results from a variety of polls to illustrate personal changes that have taken place in the lives of the millions of adults looking for self-fulfillment and development, Yankelovich draws vivid portraits of their experiments as they revolt against some of the old values and ethics in their search for new rules for living.

Betty Menson is director of adult learning services at Ohio University.

Index

A

Adult, defined, 14
Adult development: educational issues and, 117–120; and educative environment, 7–13; in graduate education, 45–63; implications of, for higher education, 21, 24–27; institutional responses to, 25; learning related to, 7–30; life cycle phases and developmental stages in, 14–21; and professional socialization, 50–54; research needed on, 118; themes and issues in, 14–15; and transitions, 10, 15–17, 24; and women students, 31–43
Adult education: educational brokering for, 75–85; institutional commitment to, 119; principles for, 119–120
Adulthood, defined, 14
American Association of Law Schools, 45n
Andragogy, pedagogy compared with, 11–12
Antioch New England Graduate School, 45n; Clinical Supervision Group at, 58; Department of Professional Psychology at, 47, 55–60; Professional Seminar at, 57, 59–60; Role Relations Seminar at, 57–58; Theme-Centered Group at, 58–59
Arbeiter, S., 121
Aslanian, C. B., 33, 42, 121
Association of American Colleges, 121

B

Bach, R., 97
Baltes, P., 15, 21, 28
Bart, P. B., 33, 43
Blum, L., 43
Bolles, R., 3, 4
Boston, women's program in, 38
Brickell, H. M., 33, 42, 121

Bucher, R., 48, 62
Bureau of Labor Statistics, 3, 4

C

Canfield, J., 92, 97
Center for Holistic Education, 92, 94
Chickering, A. W., 2, 5, 7–30, 70, 117, 119, 120, 121
Chiriboga, D., 33, 43, 123
Cincinnati, educational brokering in, 76–85
Cincinnati, University of, Raymond Walters College of, 83
Cincinnati Technical College, 79
Clark, R., 48, 62
Clark, T., 24, 28
Cohn, R., 57
College Park, Maryland, women's program in, 39
Columbia Law School, 61
Compact for Lifelong Educational Opportunities (CLEO), 115
Coppedge, F. L., 120
Coulter, W., 57, 62
Council for the Advancement of Experiential Learning (CAEL), 62; Project LEARN of, 72
Counselors, for educational brokering, 84–85
Credit for Lifelong Learning (CLL): and experiential process, 93–97; group approach to, 90–93; holistic techniques for, 87–98; and student characteristics, 88–90
Cross, K. P., 1, 5, 8–11, 14, 15, 16, 17, 18–19, 21, 28, 75, 85, 117, 121–122
Cytrynbaum, S., 32, 33, 43

D

Daly, J. J., 34, 43
Darrow, C. N., 29, 62
Department of Labor, 79, 85
Detroit, women's program in, 39
Deutscher, I., 34, 43

Widick, C., 11, 17, 30
Wilk, C., 43
Winn, H. D., 34, 43
Wollitzer, P., 123
Women: as adult students, 31–43, 82–83; characteristics of, 32–34; checklist for institutional response to, 40–41; and empty-nest period, 33–34; issues for, 31–32, 41–42; motivations of, 33–34; problems of, 36; programs and services for, 34–35, 38–39; self-concept of, 34; support networks for, 34, 35–38, 42, 82; terms for, 31; and transitions, 33, 50, 52–53

Women's Opportunities Network (WON): goals and objectives of, 35–36; influences of, 37–38; orientation program by, 36–37; survey results for, 36

Workers. *See* Service economy workers

Y

Yale Law School, 46
Yankelovich, D., 124